WONDER WOMAN

AMAZON WARRIOR

By Steve Korté

Illustrated by Marcus To

Wonder Woman created by William Moulton Marston

SCHOLASTIC INC.

BACKSTORIES

Copyright © 2016 DC Comics. WONDER WOMAN and all related characters and elements are trademarks of and © DC Comics. (s16)
SCUS36035

ISBN 978-0-545-92557-0

10 9 8 7 6 5 4 3 2 1   16 17 18 19 20

Printed in the U.S.A.   40
First printing 2016

Book design by Rick DeMonico

CONTENTS

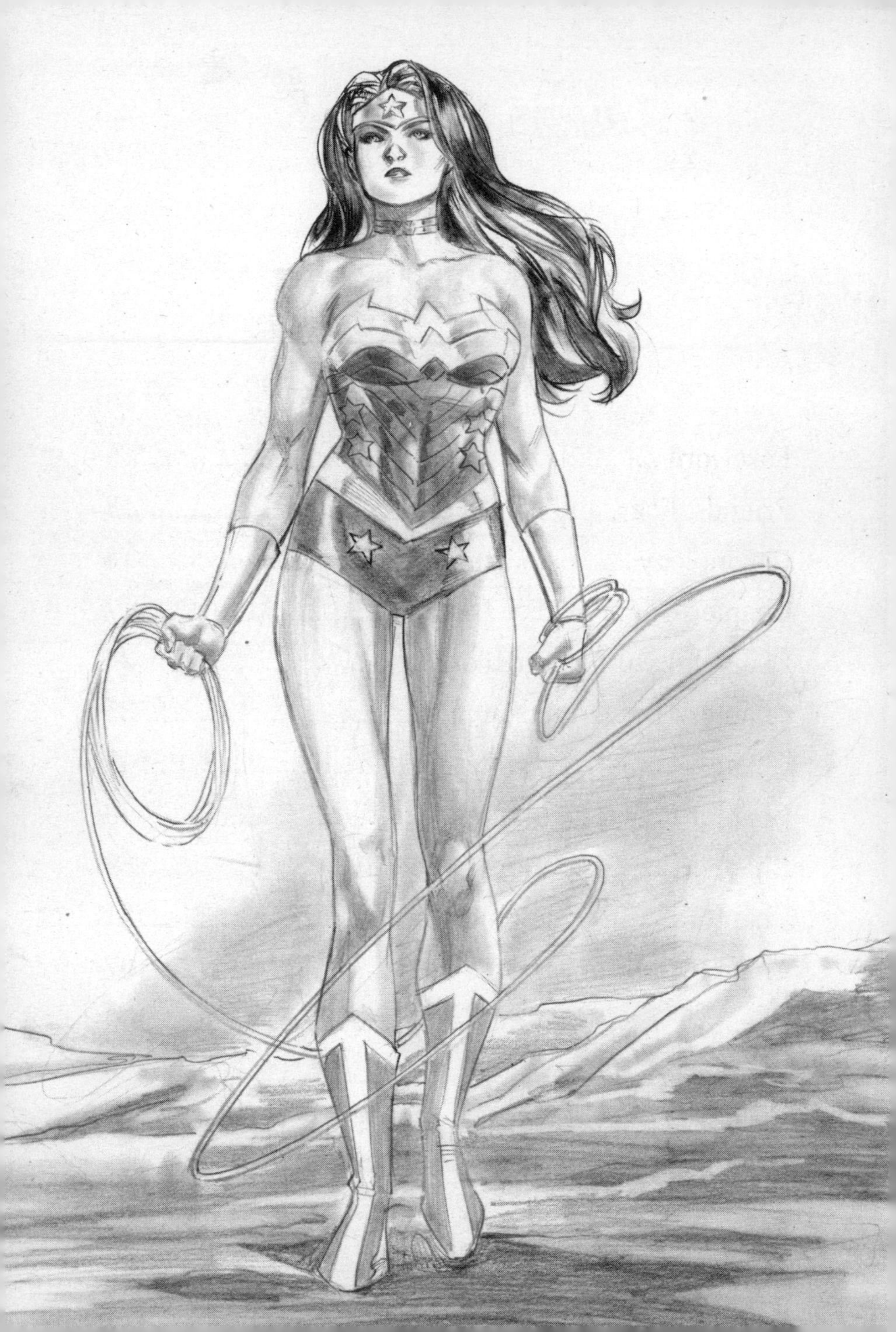

Foreword
by Wonder Woman

You know me as Wonder Woman. Perhaps you also know me as Princess Diana of the Amazons. Yet I wonder if you know my real story. Did you know that you and I are from different worlds?

I come from a line of mighty women known as the Amazons who live on a faraway island called Themyscira. Some have also called my home "Paradise Island." My beloved mother is Hippolyta, the Queen of the Amazons.

Although I was the daughter of a queen and lived in the royal palace, I always tried to forget that

I was a princess. I spent the happiest days of my childhood running through the forests on my island or hunting with a bow and arrow.

The Amazons are brave warriors, and I was raised to be a skilled fighter. However, my mother and my fellow Amazons also taught me that there is something mightier than violence. That is the power of peace.

Years ago, your world was facing a dangerous threat that would have meant the destruction of all human beings. I was chosen by the Amazons of Themyscira to journey to your world and face that threat. Yet that was only part of my mission. I was also sent to your world to teach the Amazonian ways of harmony. I came to give hope to those who are without hope and bring justice to those who facing evil. Most of all, I was sent to teach the Amazon philosophy of peace and equality for all.

Love and compassion are the two words that guide my life. I know that your world can be cruel, and sometimes it can be hard and harsh. I want to try to make it a better world.

On Themyscira, our stonemason crafted a giant tablet on which she carved the "Code of the Amazons." Here is what it says:

"Let all who read these words know that we are a nation of women, dedicated to our sisters, and to the peace that is humankind's right. We have been gifted with the mission to unite the people of our world with love and compassion. We are dedicated to the ideals of uniting all people, all sexes, and all creeds. We will overcome hatred with love. We are the Amazons, and we have come to save mankind."

Friends, Foes, and Family

Wonder Woman

Diana was the first child born on Themyscira, and she was also the island's first princess. She was born with amazing powers of strength and speed, and she is a superb warrior. As Wonder Woman, she has joined our world to fight evildoers and spread a message of peace.

Hippolyta

Hippolyta is the Queen of the Amazons and mother of Princess Diana. She has lived for over 3,000 years. Like all Amazons, she is a skilled warrior. She is also a wise ruler and a loving mother.

General Phillipus

It was Amazon General
Phillipus who trained Diana in
the art of combat and taught
the princess how to use her
incredible powers. She is
Queen Hippolyta's most trusted
advisor.

Antiope

Antiope was the sister of Queen
Hippolyta, and she was also a
queen. She ruled a separate
tribe of Amazons known as the
Bana-Mighdall, who chose to
live in Egypt.

Artemis

Artemis is the daughter of Queen Antiope, and she is Diana's friend and occasional rival. Artemis is a brave warrior, possessing great strength and keen archery skills. She also has a quick temper, which can get her into trouble.

Diana Trevor

Test pilot Diana Trevor crashed her plane near Themyscira and was nursed back to health by the Amazons. Trevor later became a hero when she lost her life fighting alongside the Amazons.

Steve Trevor

Steve Trevor is the only son of Diana Trevor, and like his mother he found himself on Themyscira. He was the first mortal man to set foot on the island. When Princess Diana journeyed to the outside world, one of her missions was to bring Trevor back to America.

Donna Troy

Donna was a magical twin of Diana, created as a playmate for the young princess on Paradise Island. Tragedy struck early in Donna's life when she was kidnapped, and it has taken her years to recover from that terrible event.

Ares

Ares is the God of War, and he is one of Wonder Woman's most dangerous enemies. He has nearly unlimited power to control humans. Ares loves war and conflict, and he hates the Amazons. He has vowed to destroy them.

Cheetah

Dr. Barbara Minerva is an archaeologist who ate a strange, ancient plant, hoping that it would give her immortality. Instead, it transformed her into the Cheetah: a ferocious feline with great strength and razor-sharp claws.

Circe

Circe is a powerful sorceress, who has been plotting against the Amazons for centuries. She has almost unlimited magical powers, including the ability to transform men into animals.

Giganta

Dr. Doris Zeul was the victim of a scientific experiment that went terribly wrong and turned her into the giant villain Giganta. She towers one hundred feet above Wonder Woman and possesses the strength of several hundred gorillas, making her a mighty foe.

Chronology

The Amazons were a race of brave women that lived apart from the rest of mankind on a secret island called Themyscira.

The greatest foe of the Amazons was Ares, the fierce God of War.

Diana Trevor crash-landed on Themyscira and gave her life protecting the Amazons.

Ares declared war on the rest of the world, and Hippolyta decided that one Amazon would leave Themyscira to battle Ares and also escort Steve Trevor back to Man's World.

A great contest was announced to choose the Amazon who would fight Ares. Hippolyta would not let Diana enter the contest, so Diana disguised herself.

After Diana defeated all the other Amazons in the contest, her mother reluctantly agreed that Diana should travel to Man's World.

Queen Hippolyta, the leader of the Amazons, longed to have a child. Her wish was granted, and she gave birth to a daughter, Diana.

Princess Diana possessed great strength and soon became a mighty warrior.

Air Force pilot Steve Trevor became the first man to visit Themyscira after his jet crashed nearby.

Diana put on a star-spangled uniform and left Themyscira to battle Ares.

She defeated Ares before he was able to destroy mankind.

Diana decided to stay in Man's World to fight for truth and justice. In her new role as protector of mankind, she became known as the mighty hero Wonder Woman!

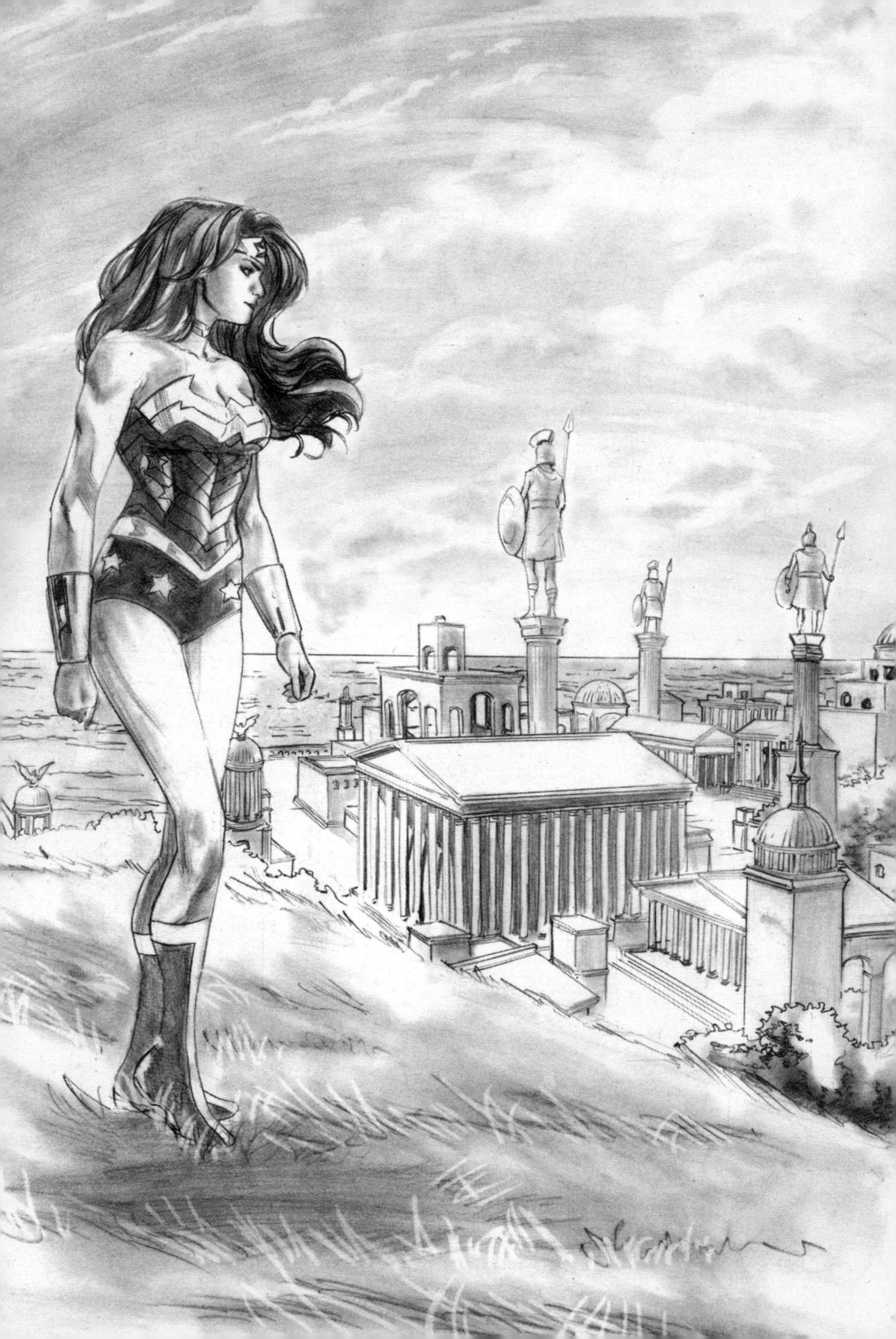

CHAPTER ONE

PARADISE ISLAND

Centuries ago, there were Greek gods who lived on Mount Olympus and were led by Zeus. These gods created a race of mighty women known as the Amazons. The gods hoped that the Amazons would inspire the rest of the world to pursue truth and justice. One god was very unhappy that the Amazons had been created. He was Ares, the son of Zeus. Ares was also known as the God of War.

Two queens, Hippolyta and her sister, Antiope, ruled the Amazons in the faraway city of Themyscira.

Although the Amazons were strong warriors, they chose to live quietly. Their only desire was to live in peaceful harmony. But Ares had other ideas. He convinced Heracles, who was one of the strongest gods on Mount Olympus, that the Amazons should be conquered. Heracles formed an army and attacked Themyscira, destroying the city.

Hippolyta and Antiope

Hippolyta and her sister, Antiope, were created by the
Greek gods centuries ago. Although the two women ruled
the Amazons together for many years, they were not alike.
Hippolyta was calmer than her sister and valued peace.
Antiope had a quick temper and was sometimes too eager
to battle her enemies.

Half of the Amazons, led by Antiope, cried out for revenge and chose to pursue Heracles. They were determined to defeat his army. The rest of the Amazons stayed with Queen Hippolyta. Instead of seeking revenge, they traveled far away to create a new home on a secret tropical island. There they could establish a perfect, peaceful society, separating themselves from "Man's World," as they called the rest of mankind.

The Amazons still called their new island home Themyscira, but it was so beautiful that some also called it "Paradise Island." The Greek goddess Athena rewarded the Amazons for choosing to live peacefully and granted them the power to live forever on their island, undisturbed by any mortal humans. The Amazons continued to train as warriors, but they hoped that they would never have to put their fighting skills to use. Their only duty was to guard Doom's Doorway, which was a sealed door on Themyscira. Behind that door was a tunnel where

THE SEALED GATEWAY KNOWN AS DOOM'S DOORWAY IS MADE OF TWELVE LAYERS OF THE STRONGEST AMAZONIAN STEEL.

some of the world's most dangerous monsters were chained far below the island.

For over 3,000 years, the Amazons lived undisturbed on Themyscira. Sometimes, though, mortals did visit the island. The first time it happened

THE BEAUTIFUL BEACHES OF THEMYSCIRA ALSO PROTECT THE AMAZONS FROM THE OUTSIDE WORLD.

was when an American test pilot named Diana Trevor parachuted into the waters near Themyscira after a lightning bolt destroyed her plane. Trevor was badly injured, but the Amazons took her to their nearby Isle of Healing and nursed her back to health.

Not long after Trevor had recovered, a terrible creature called Cottus broke free from its chains within the Pits of Tartarus and smashed through Doom's Doorway.

Cottus was a giant monster with one hundred arms. Years of imprisonment had fueled its hatred of the Amazons.

Just as Cottus was about to attack, Diana Trevor came to the rescue. She led the beast down the shore and away from the city, distracting the creature until the Amazons could capture it. The Amazons were saved,

THIS PATCH SHOWING THE AMERICAN FLAG WAS ON DIANA TREVOR'S FLIGHT JACKET.

Doom's Doorway

On a secluded spot on Paradise Island, two Amazons always stood guard outside a giant metal door known as Doom's Doorway. A tunnel behind the door led to the Pits of Tartarus, where many of the most horrible creatures who had ever lived were imprisoned. Two of the most evil were the seven-headed dragon called the Hydra and the fire-breathing beast known as the Chimera.

but Diana Trevor was crushed by Cottus during the battle and lost her own life. The Amazons built a mighty statue to honor Diana Trevor. Years later, her name would be given in honor to the most famous Amazon ever.

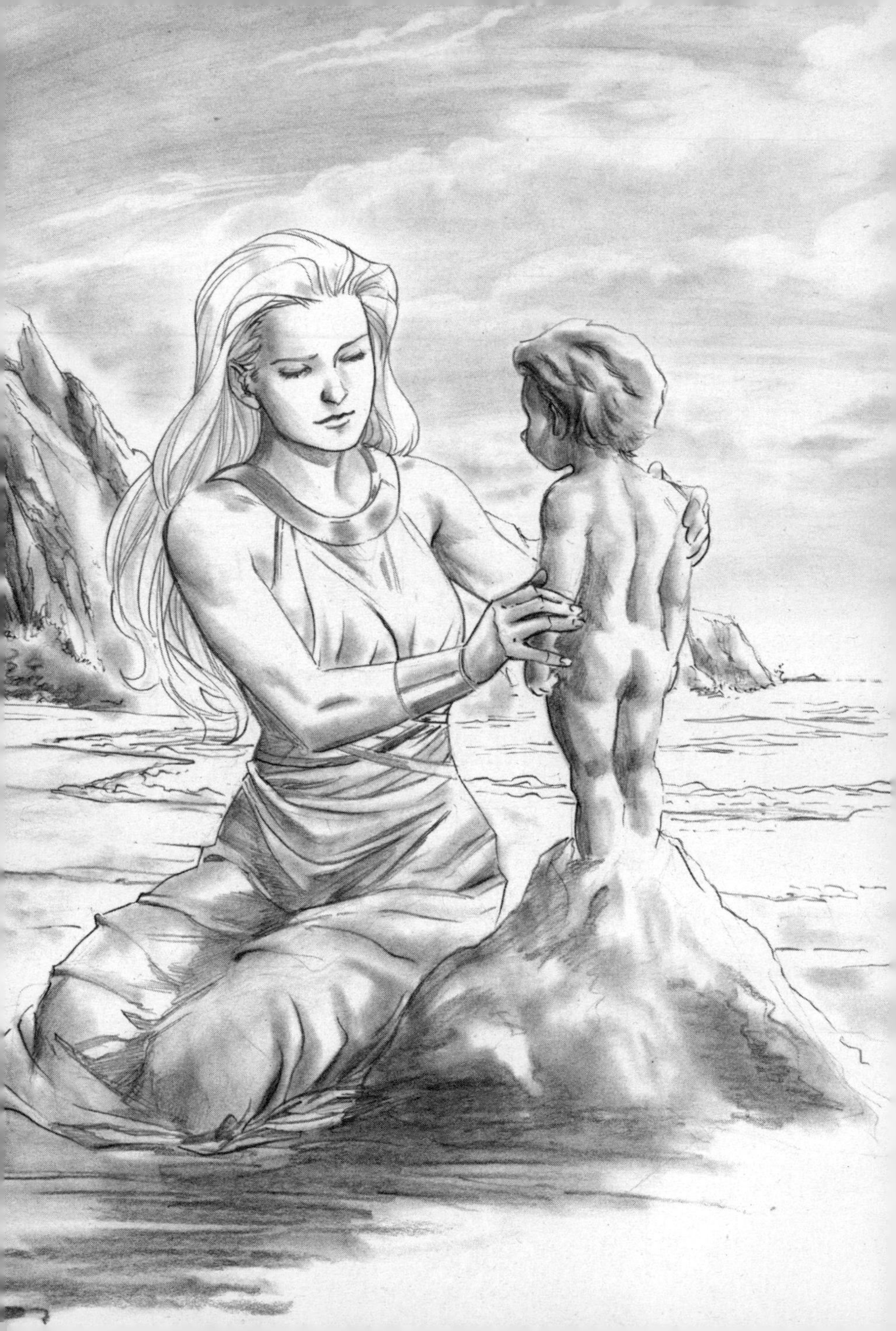

CHAPTER TWO

THE BIRTH OF DIANA

The Amazons on Themyscira were grown women, and there were no children on the island. For 3,000 years, Queen Hippolyta had longed to have a child of her own, but that seemed to be an impossible dream. One day, Hippolyta met with an Amazon named Menalippe, and the queen spoke of her wish for a child.

Menalippe had the power to talk with the Greek gods, and she told Hippolyta that it was possible for her to have a child. First, she told Hippolyta to go to the beach and kneel in the sand. There she was to gather together clay from the ground of the island and sculpt it into the shape of a child. And then Hippolyta was told to wait for a miracle.

Far above Themyscira and hidden within the clouds was Mount Olympus, the home of the gods and goddesses. Five of them looked down at Hippolyta. They decided to grant her request and gave life to

ARTEMIS, HERMES, APHRODITE, ATHENA, AND DEMETER LOOKED DOWN IN MERCY ON HIPPOLYTA.

Menalippe

Menalippe was one of the wisest women on Themyscira, and Queen Hippolyta often went to her for advice. Menalippe had the power to predict future events, and could communicate directly with the gods.

the clay sculpture. This little girl was the first child ever to be born on Paradise Island!

Each goddess and god gave a special quality to the newborn girl. Athena granted wisdom; Demeter gave power and great strength; Aphrodite gave beauty and a loving heart; Hermes granted the powers of flight and speed; and Artemis gave the

MENALIPPE WAS ABLE TO SEE INTO THE FUTURE WHEN SHE GAZED INTO THIS POOL OF WATER ON THEMYSCIRA.

HIPPOLYTA THANKED THE GODS FOR HER MIRACULOUS DAUGHTER.

power to communicate with animals and the skills of a great huntress.

Hippolyta was overjoyed when her daughter raised her arms and cried out for her mother. She hugged the child close to her. With a smile, Hippolyta remembered the brave test pilot Diana Trevor, who had given her life to save the Amazons.

"I am going to name you Diana," she said to the child who was now sleeping peacefully in her arms.

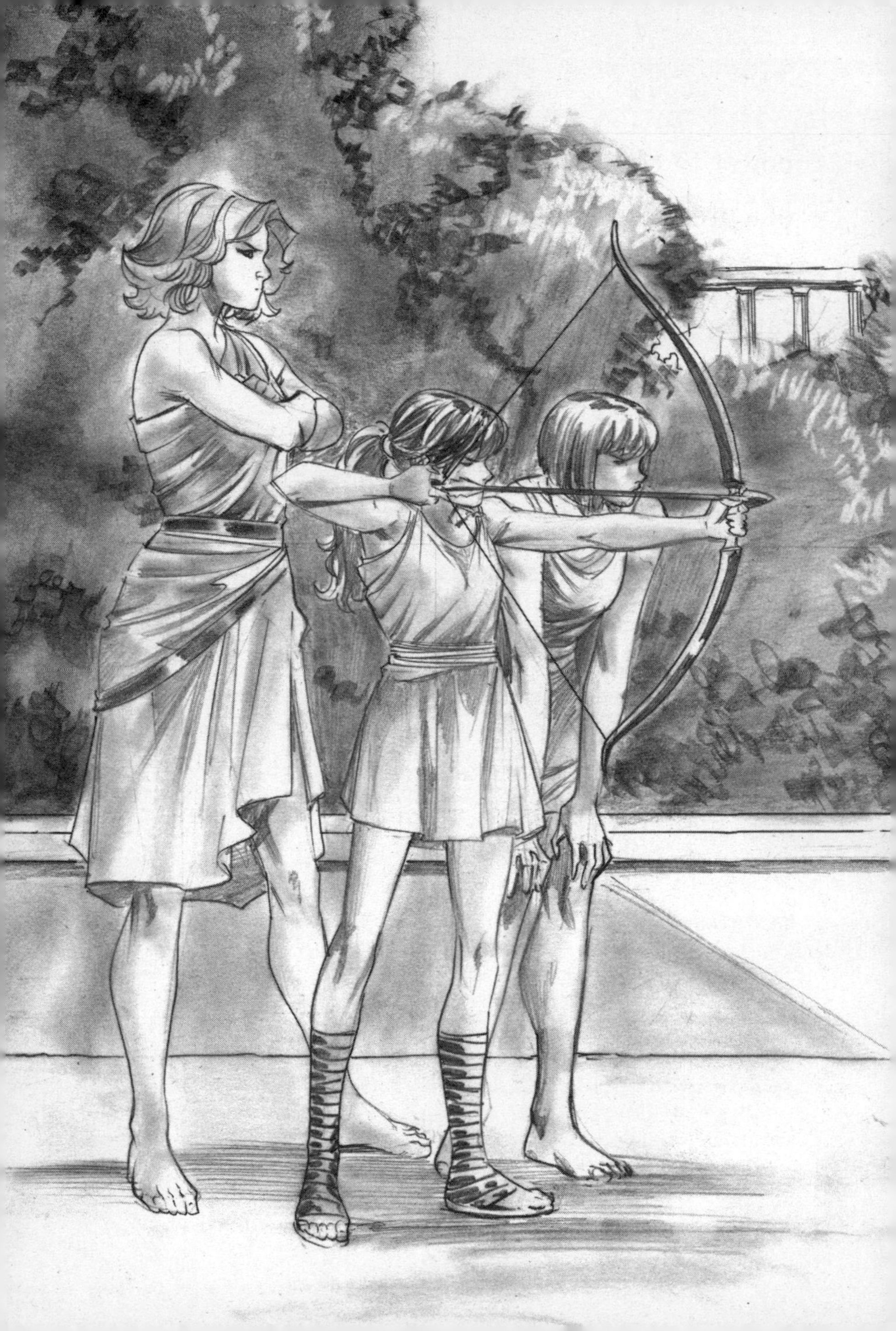

CHAPTER THREE

AMAZON LIFE

Princess Diana was the first child to be born on Themyscira. Growing up, Diana was surrounded by a thousand Amazons who loved her and wanted to guide her. The Amazons consulted ancient books on raising children and took turns watching over the princess in the royal palace. They soon discovered that what made Diana happiest of all were those rare days when her mother permitted her to leave the white marble towers of the palace. Diana would joyfully spend the entire day

exploring the forests and beaches of Paradise Island.

By the age of five, Diana had decided that life in the palace was quiet and restful and definitely boring. She would try to entertain herself by jumping from one marble step to another, waving her wooden sword in the air.

Hippolyta would watch her child playing and sigh. She knew that the gods had given mighty powers to her headstrong daughter. Hippolyta was worried that Diana would have trouble controlling those powers.

Even as a small child, Diana was able to demonstrate the great strength that had been granted to her by the goddess Demeter. Diana could lift a giant oak tree with her bare hands. She could swim faster than the dolphins in the ocean.

WHEN FACED WITH A DIFFICULT TASK, DIANA OFTEN CALLS UPON THE GODS FOR HELP.

General Phillipus

General Phillipus was a brave and strong soldier who
trained Princess Diana in the art of combat. When the
Amazons first moved to the island of Themyscira, it was
General Phillipus who built the mighty Doom's Doorway to
keep the monsters of the world locked out of sight.

And one time she managed to wrestle a wild boar to the ground. That night, Diana came back to the palace with her clothes torn and her long black hair all in tangles.

"It was the best day *ever!*" she said happily to her mother.

Hippolyta looked at her daughter in exasperation.

Following the ancient Amazonian tradition, Diana was raised as a warrior. She became an expert with a sword and bow, and soon she mastered all

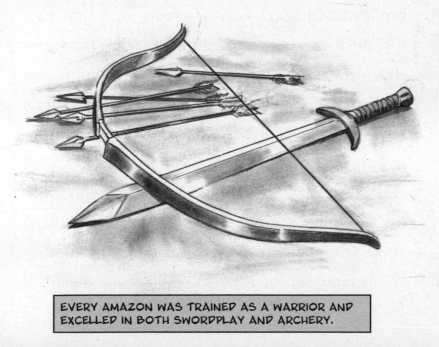

EVERY AMAZON WAS TRAINED AS A WARRIOR AND EXCELLED IN BOTH SWORDPLAY AND ARCHERY.

the martial arts. At the age of seven, Diana started combat training with General Phillipus, the Amazons' greatest warrior. Phillipus encouraged the princess to resolve her problems peacefully, but that wasn't always an easy lesson for Diana to learn. With her special powers, Diana began to feel invulnerable. She even started to resent her mother for being too protective of her.

By the time Diana was a teenager, Hippolyta was worried that her daughter was growing too confident in her warrior skills and ignoring the Amazon code of finding peaceful solutions. Hippolyta consulted with General Phillipus, and they came up with a plan. One night, the general sent a group of twelve masked Amazons to confront the princess. Diana's first reaction was to lash out at the intruders, knocking them to the ground with her fists and battering them with her shield. Diana stood triumphantly over her victims, until they slowly removed their masks. Then Diana was filled

DIANA HAD TO LEARN TO CONTROL HER STRENGTH.

Ares

Ares is the son of the Greek god Zeus, and like the other gods he has mighty powers, including immortality and the ability to change his appearance. Ares uses his powers for evil, and he grows even stronger when those around him use violence. He has vowed to destroy the Amazons.

with sorrow when she realized that she had injured her fellow Amazons. She made a promise to herself to control her mighty powers and show mercy.

Not long after that, Diana was walking alone through the forest late at night. Thanks to her superb hunting skills, she heard the sound of each pine needle rustling in the trees and each chirp made by the woodland creatures. So Diana was surprised when she suddenly heard a deep voice speaking to her, "Princess, you are strong and brave. But there is one challenge you have never faced."

Diana wheeled around and was confronted by a tall man who was carrying a sword. A giant helmet covered his head, and he was dressed in dark armor.

"I am Ares, the God of War," he declared. "And I have come to teach you a lesson."

Diana had been taught to trust others, and she replied, "I wish to learn."

So Ares led Diana to a small glade within the forest. Quietly, Ares stepped back into the shadows.

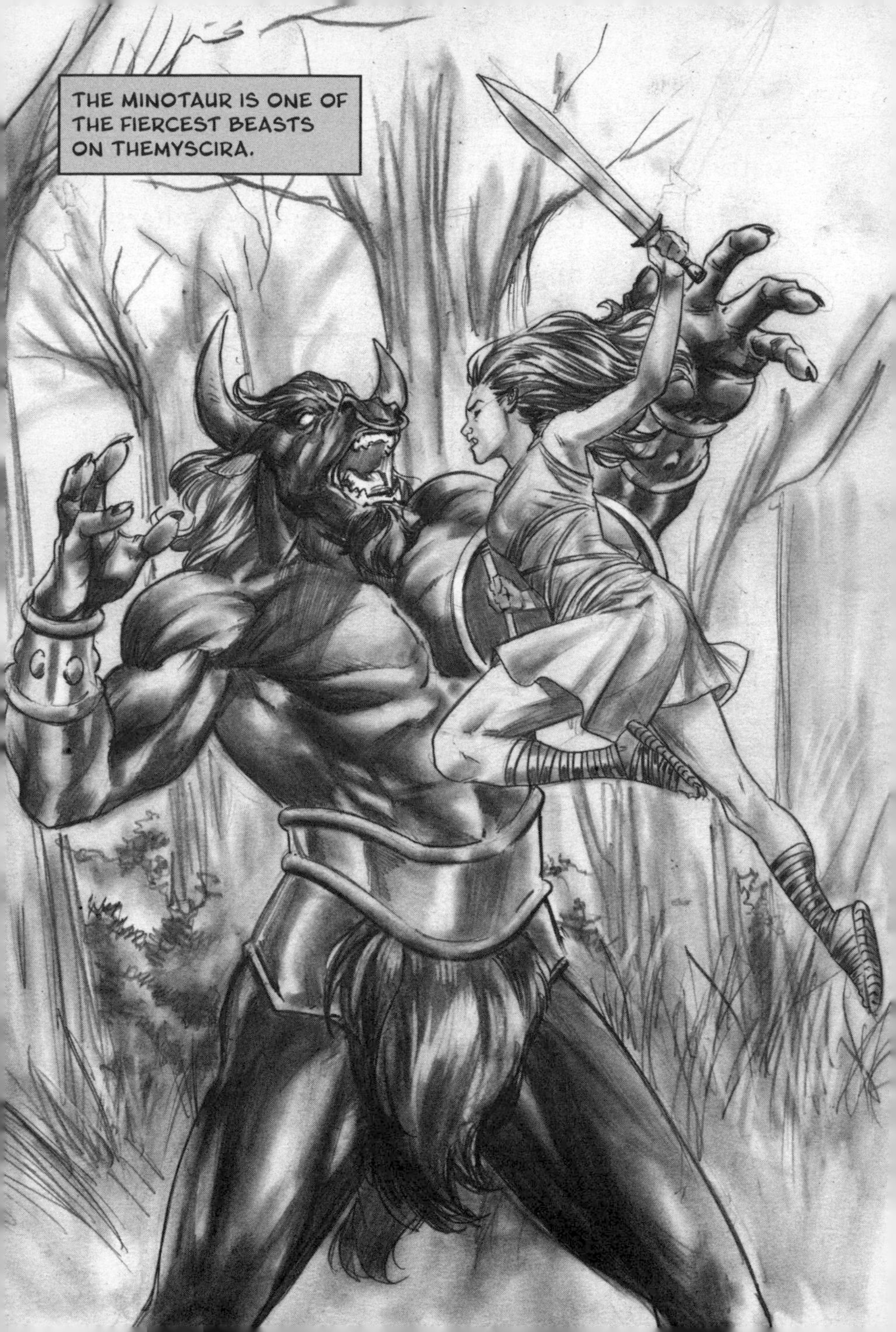
THE MINOTAUR IS ONE OF THE FIERCEST BEASTS ON THEMYSCIRA.

A giant creature with the head of a bull jumped into the glade! It was a massive creature with the head of a bull and the body of a man—the Minotaur. With a mighty roar, the monster lunged at Diana. She fought back with all her strength, but the creature knocked her to the ground.

Diana looked up in horror as the Minotaur loomed above her. Thinking quickly, she kicked out her legs, causing the monster to trip and fall over. With a thud, the Minotaur's head slammed into a tree. It fell to the ground, moaning in pain.

As Diana struggled to catch her breath, Ares stepped back into the glade.

"You are a superb warrior," Ares said. "Now it is time to finish the job. Take your sword and kill the Minotaur!"

Diana slowly raised her sword above the Minotaur, ready to end its life. But as Diana looked into the eyes of the monster, she remembered the promise she had made to herself.

"I will not kill the Minotaur," she said as she put away her sword.

"You are a fool, Diana of Themyscira!" bellowed Ares. "I can teach you nothing!"

Suddenly, with a loud crash of thunder and a blast of smoke, Ares vanished from the forest, taking the Minotaur with him.

Diana had shown compassion and mercy. She had truly become an Amazon.

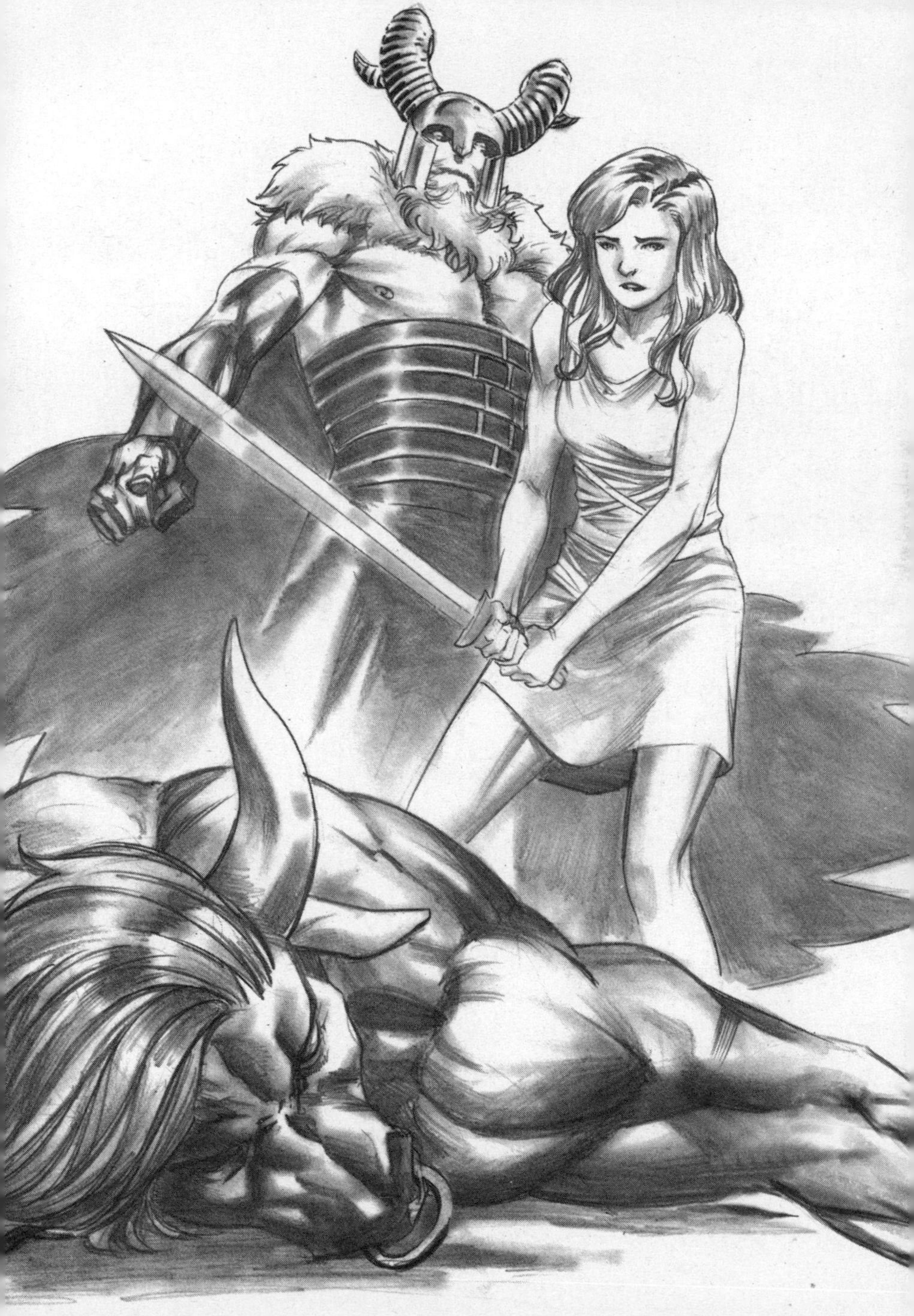

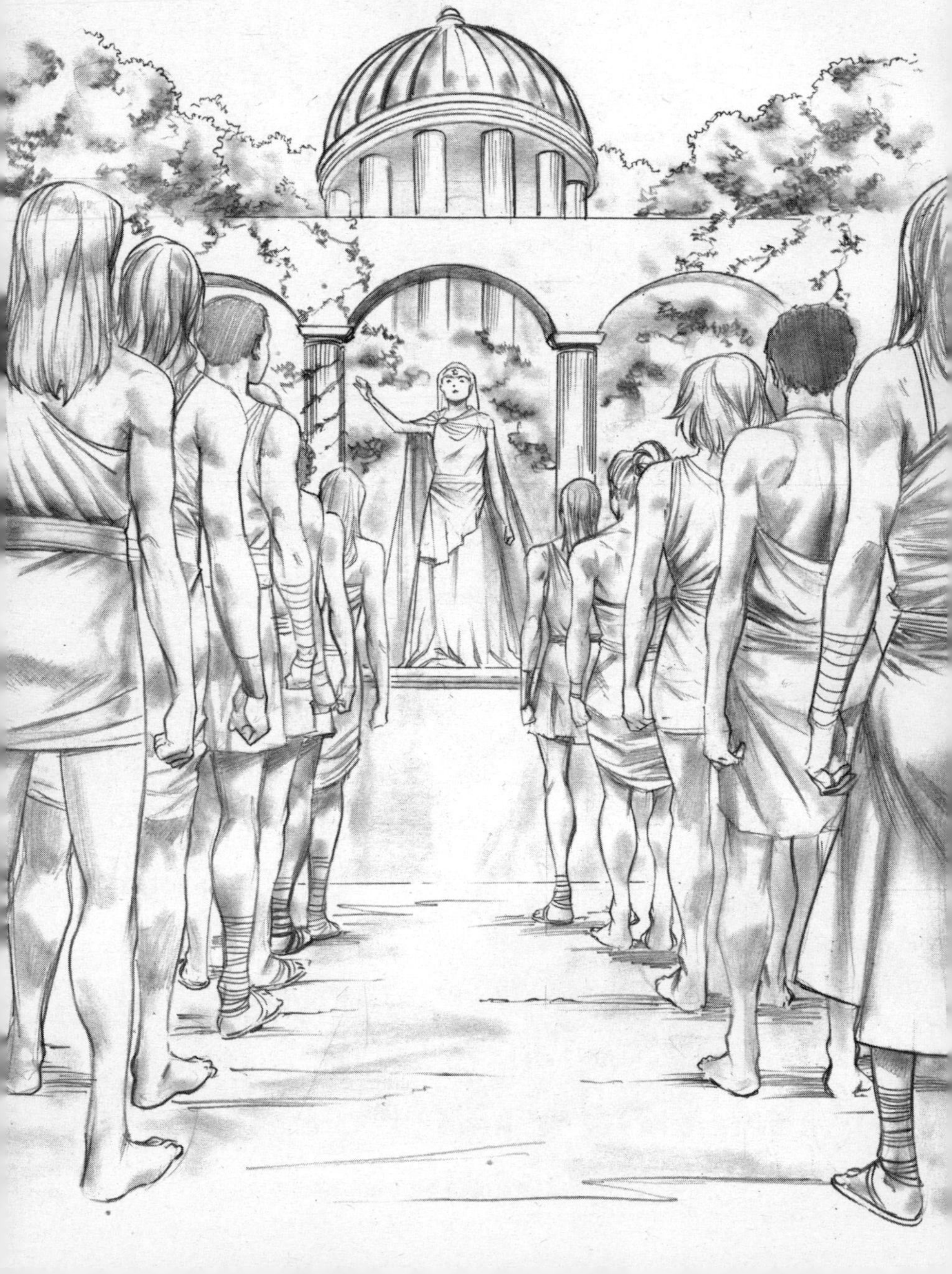

CHAPTER FOUR

THE
CONTEST

Years later, Diana's peaceful life on Themyscira was shattered when two important events occurred. First, the Amazons learned that Ares was planning a war against all of mankind. The God of War was plotting to trick two nations into firing nuclear bombs that would destroy all the humans on Earth.

The other event was the arrival of a mortal man on Paradise Island. His name was Steve Trevor, and he was a pilot in the United States Air Force. He was also the son of Diana Trevor, who had given her life fighting for the Amazons years ago. Like his mother, Steve Trevor came to Themyscira after his own plane crashed near the island. Although he was not injured, he was stranded on Paradise Island with no way to get home.

WHEN STEVE TREVOR WASHED ASHORE ON THEMYSCIRA, HE HAD NO IDEA WHERE HE WAS!

STEVE WAS ASTONISHED TO SEE THE STATUE OF HIS MOTHER THAT THE AMAZONS BUILT ON THEMYSCIRA.

Steve Trevor

Steve Trevor was the first mortal man to visit Paradise
Island after his airplane crashed in the waters surrounding
Themyscira. He was also the first man that Princess Diana
met. Trevor was a successful pilot in the United States
Air Force, and he later became a valuable ally to Wonder
Woman.

Queen Hippolyta had a plan. She would choose one Amazon to escort Steve Trevor back to America. And then that same brave warrior would try to defeat Ares. All of the Amazons were gathered outside the royal palace to hear the queen.

"A warrior is needed to challenge Ares!" she called out. "Tomorrow, we will hold a contest to find the champion who will travel to Man's World. There she will fight for the freedom of all mortal women and men."

Diana desperately wanted to stand up to Ares, and later that night she begged her mother to allow her to compete. The queen refused to consider it.

"I'm sorry, Diana," she said. "But you are the youngest of the Amazons, and this mission is too dangerous. I forbid it!"

The next day, Diana sulked in her room as the Amazons gathered in the stadium.

"This is so unfair," she grumbled to herself. "If I could just prove to mother how strong and brave I am, she would be forced to declare me the champion!" Then Diana had an idea. She jumped off her bed, grabbed a metal combat helmet that hid most of her face, and ran out of the palace toward the stadium.

Inside the arena, the contest had begun. The crowd cheered during the first event as six Amazons tried to race a deer. Suddenly, a seventh masked Amazon joined the contestants. The new arrival easily outran the other Amazons. She even outran the deer!

DIANA USED A HELMET AT THE CONTEST TO HIDE HER IDENTITY.

The masked Amazon then won the archery event by hitting a perfect bull's-eye with each arrow. She won the javelin throwing and long-jump contests, and she managed to push a giant boulder farther than any other contestant. At the end of the competition, the masked Amazon had defeated all her opponents.

"Worthy Amazon, you are the champion," Hippolyta announced. "Please remove your mask."

The queen and crowd all gasped when the Amazon revealed herself as Princess Diana. Hippolyta felt a mixture of pride and fear as she realized that she would now have no choice but to allow her daughter to travel to Man's World.

Hundreds of Amazons in the stadium were cheering for the princess, but Diana was worried about her mother's reaction. She didn't have to worry long. Queen Hippolyta slowly walked down to her daughter, opened her arms, and hugged Diana tightly to her.

"The gods have given great gifts of strength and wisdom to my daughter," Hippolyta called out to the crowd. "From this day forward, Diana will forever be known as the Champion of the Amazons!"

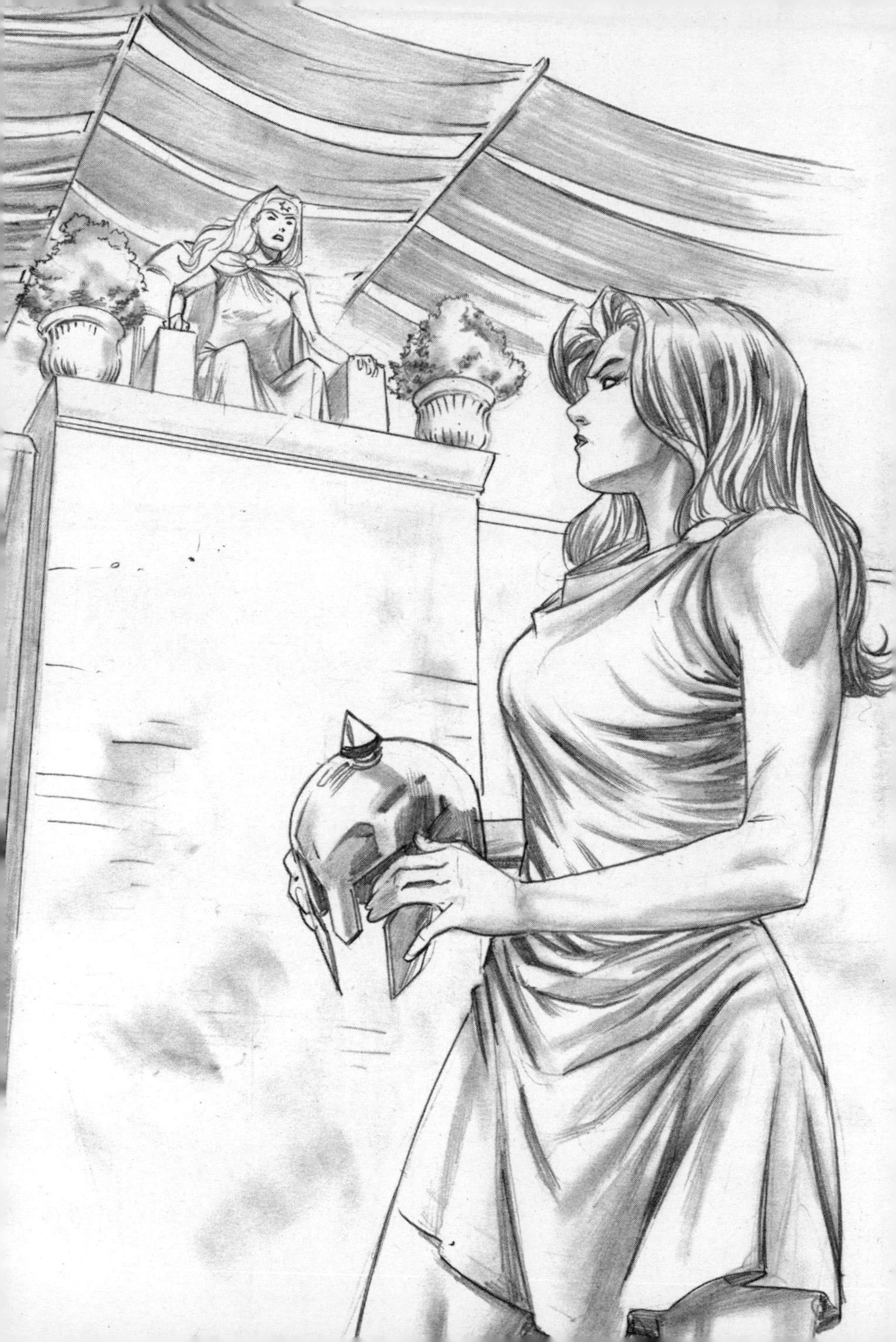

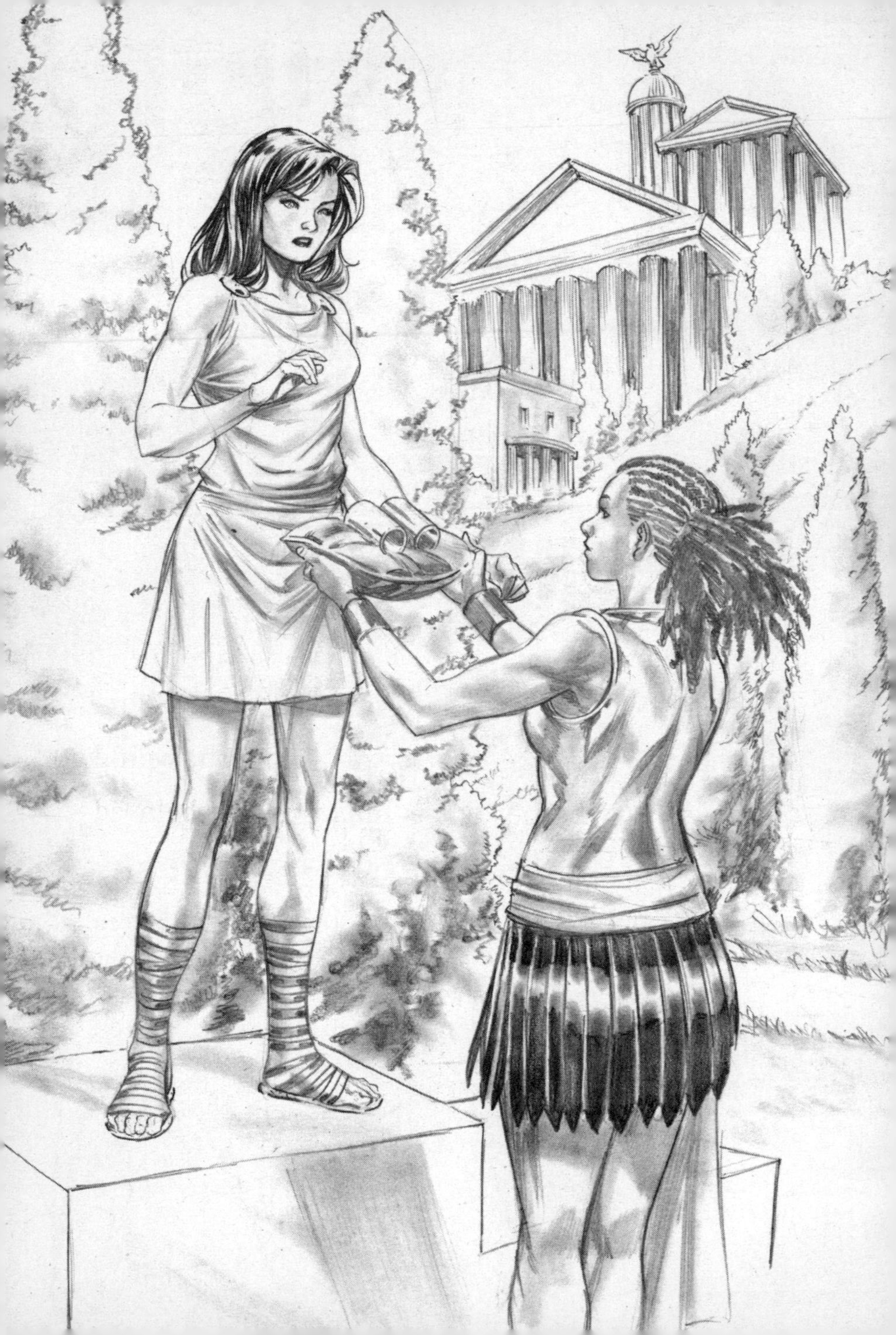

CHAPTER FIVE

THE CHAMPION

Diana smiled and waved to the cheering crowd, but she was also sad. Soon, she would be leaving her fellow Amazons and beloved island home. Who knew if she would ever return?

The crowd quieted as General Phillipus stepped forward. She was the Amazon who had trained Diana to become an expert fighter. Phillipus carried a velvet pillow in her arms, and on top of the pillow was a pair of shiny, silver bracelets.

"Princess Diana," said General Phillipus, "these

DIANA'S SILVER BRACELETS WERE FORGED FROM PIECES OF ZEUS'S SHIELD, MAKING THEM INCREDIBLY STRONG. EVEN BULLETS FIRED FROM A GUN WILL BOUNCE OFF THE BRACELETS. WHEN STRUCK TOGETHER, THEY PRODUCE A DEAFENING SOUND.

bracelets are your reward for winning the contest today."

As Diana slipped the bracelets over her wrists, Phillipus explained, "They were crafted by the god Hephaestus from mighty Zeus's shield. They are unbreakable and will serve you well in Man's World."

The next Amazon to greet Diana was the blacksmith Pallas, who held in her hands a glittering, golden suit of armor. The image of a mighty eagle had been carved into the front of the armor, and large, flexible wings were attached to the back.

PALLAS' GIFT OF ARMOR WOULD PROTECT DIANA FROM HER STRONGEST FOES.

"I crafted this battle armor for today's champion," Pallas said. "These golden wings will be helpful when you need to fly and will also protect you from danger. May this suit of armor always protect you in Man's World."

There were two more gifts for Diana, and Queen Hippolyta stepped forward to present them to her daughter. In her hands, the queen carried a large, tangled pile of golden rope and a brightly colored uniform.

"First, my beloved daughter," said Hippolyta, "I give you the Lasso of Truth."

Diana accepted the shimmering rope and was surprised at how light it felt in her hands. The rope even seemed to have a life of its own. As Diana watched in amazement, the rope quickly untangled itself and formed six oval-shaped coils.

Hippolyta explained, "This lasso comes from the goddess Hestia and was crafted by Hephaestus on Mount Olympus. It is one of the most valuable gifts

DIANA'S GOLDEN BATTLE ARMOR PROVIDES PROTECTION FROM GUNFIRE, ELECTRICITY, AND MOST EXPLOSIONS. THE EAGLE-SHAPED HELMET HAS A RETRACTABLE AND AIRTIGHT FACEPLATE.

an Amazon can receive. The lasso is made of pure gold and cannot be cut. Most important of all, it forces anyone within its bonds to tell the truth. Use it wisely, my daughter."

Diana was awed by her gifts, but there was one more to come. Queen Hippolyta handed her daughter a star-spangled outfit that was composed of red, white, blue, and yellow fabrics.

"Years before you were born, a pilot from the United States named Diana Trevor died as a hero

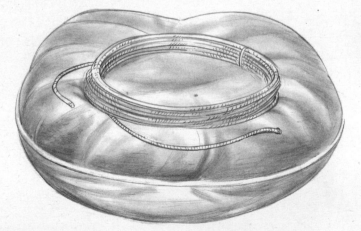

NOT ONLY DOES THE GOLDEN LASSO FORCE ANYONE COILED WITHIN IT TO TELL THE TRUTH, BUT IT ALSO HAS THE POWER TO RESTORE LOST MEMORIES AND HYPNOTIZE PEOPLE. IT CAN EVEN CHANGE ITS LENGTH, DEPENDING ON DIANA'S NEEDS.

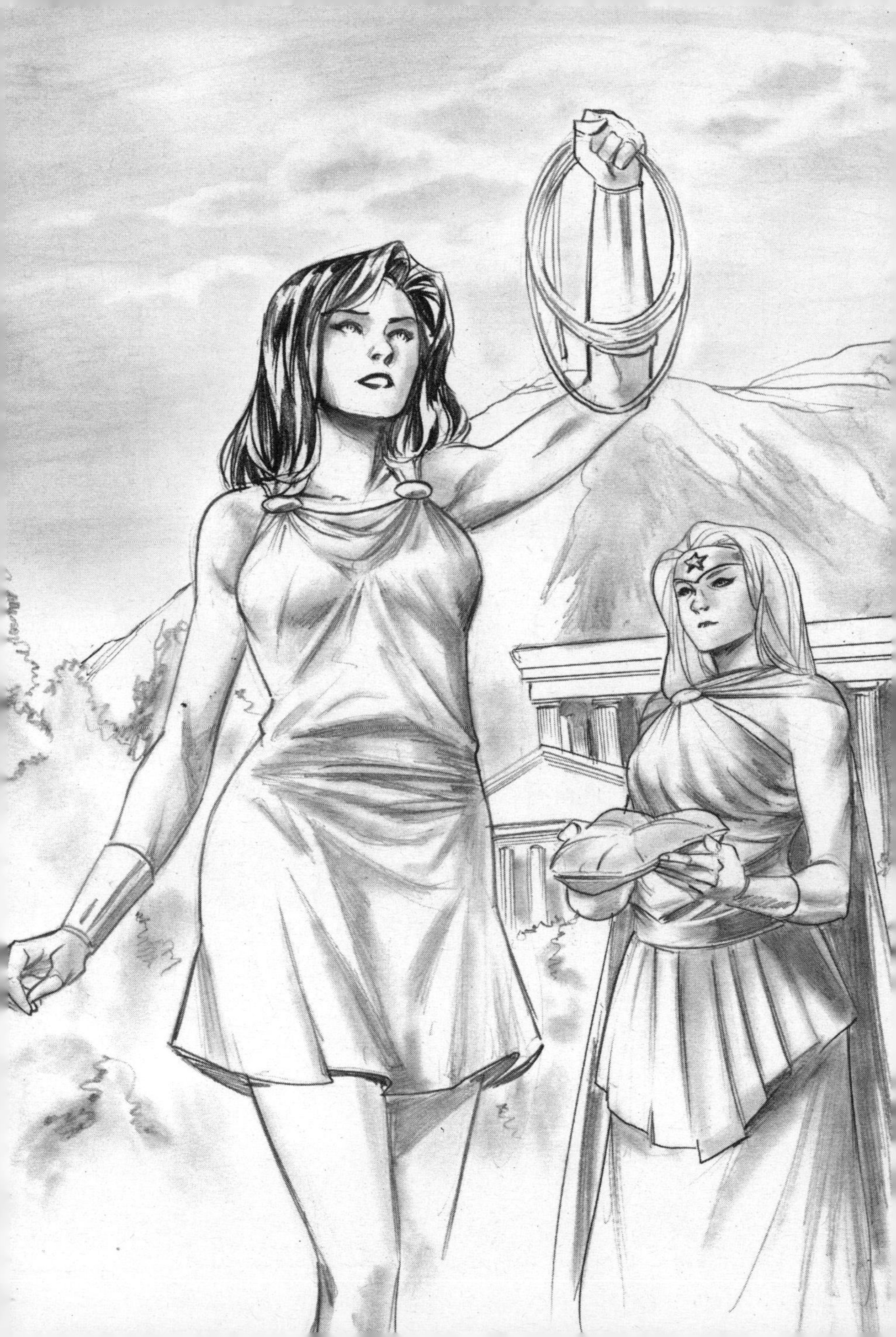

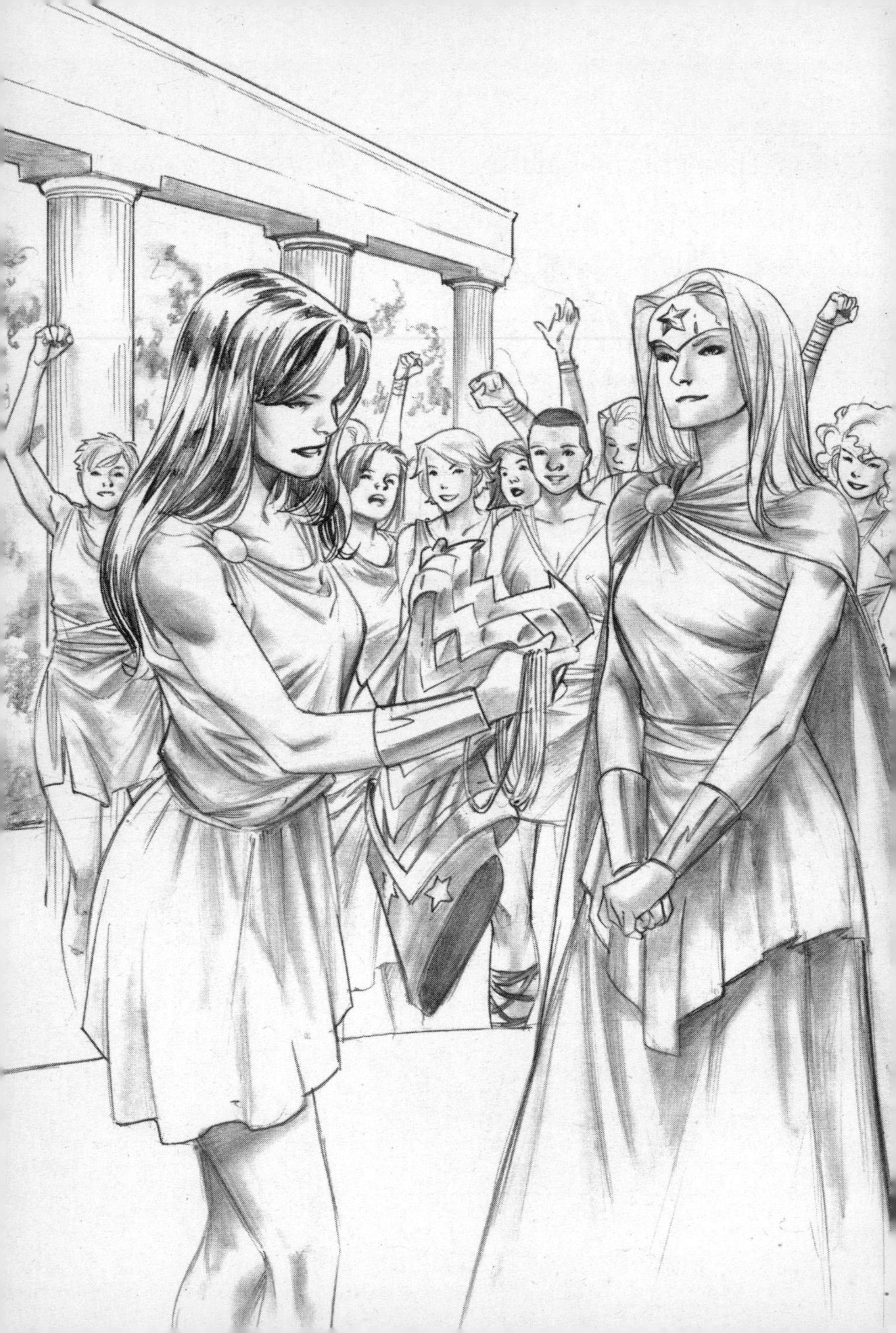

on Themyscira," said the queen. "You were named after that hero, and now you will be traveling to her world. There was a badge on Diana's flight jacket showing the flag of her country. We have created a uniform for you that was inspired by that American flag."

The princess was so overwhelmed that she could not speak. The spectators began to chant, "Diana, Diana, Diana!"

She smiled. Diana knew that the crowd was honoring both her and the brave test pilot who had given her life to protect the Amazons.

THE AMAZONS KNEW DIANA WOULD BE A GREAT CHAMPION—NOT JUST FOR THEM, BUT FOR THE WHOLE WORLD.

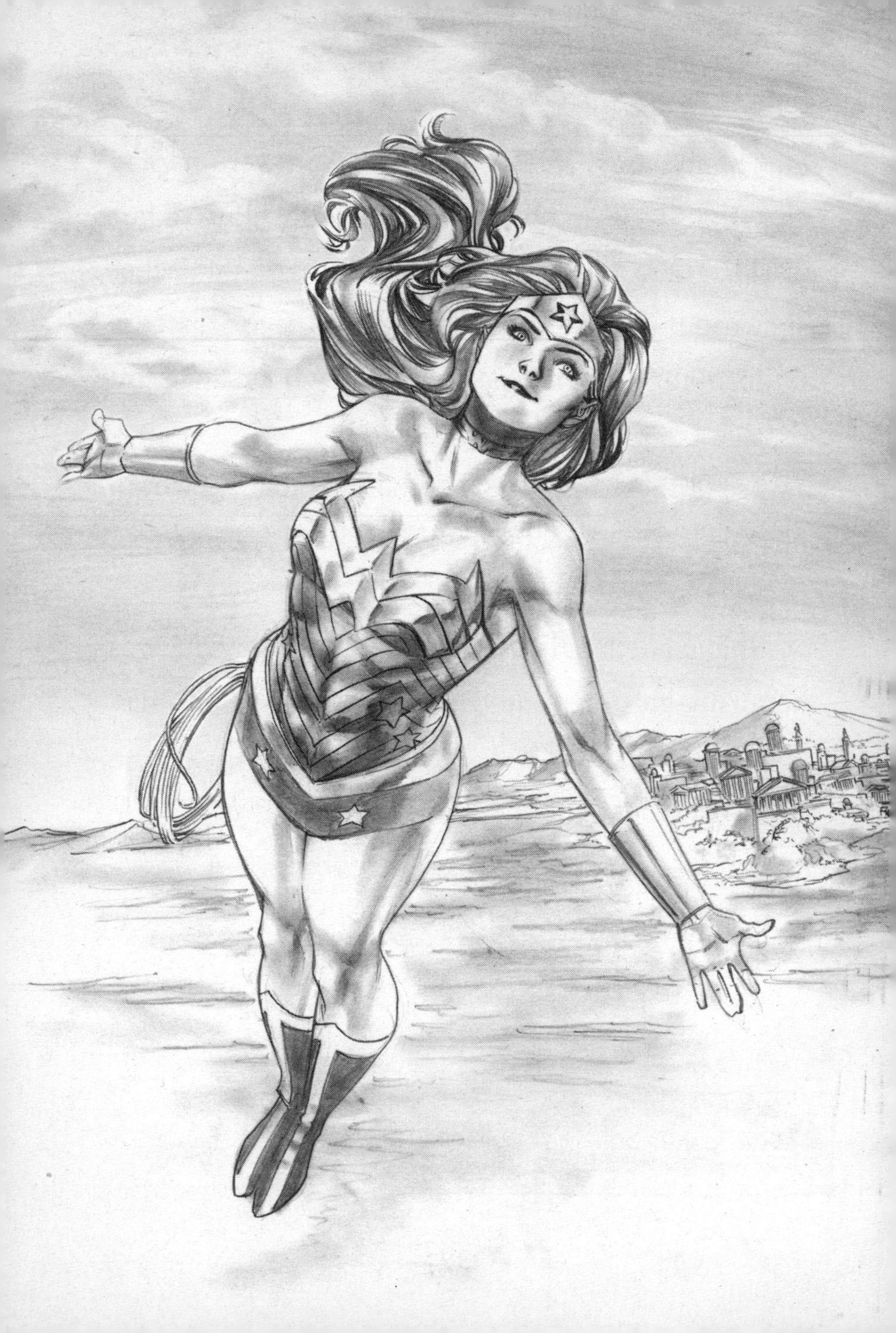

CHAPTER SIX

BECOMING
WONDER WOMAN

As the Amazons feared, Ares had grown stronger by feeding on the hatred of humans as they fought one another. Now that the God of War was at the peak of his evil powers, he planned to destroy all of mankind by starting World War III. Ares was plotting to trick two nations into launching a nuclear war that would soon escalate to include every nation on earth. No human beings could survive these nuclear explosions. After that, Ares would turn his attention to destroying the Amazons on Themyscira.

Diana's mission was to warn the mortals of Earth and try to stop Ares's plot. She was also going to escort Air Force pilot Steve Trevor back to the mortal world. Together, Diana and Trevor began their journey to the United States. It was the first time that she had ever left Paradise Island. Diana was nervous but very excited!

Their first stop was Boston, Massachusetts, where Diana returned Steve Trevor to his apartment. As Diana stood on the sidewalk outside his building, she was amazed to see how different Man's World was from Themyscira. The buildings were crammed closely together and composed of dark stone and steel, unlike the gleaming white marble structures on Paradise Island. She walked to the edge of a nearby harbor, but no one was swimming, probably because the water was so filthy.

The people near Diana moved quickly, either walking or traveling in their vehicles, and they

never seemed to stop to look at one another. She did notice that some mortal men and women stopped to stare at her, but when she opened her arms and tried to offer a hug, which was the way that all Amazons greeted one another, the humans ignored her.

Boston

WEATHER
Partly cloudy, chance of
showers tomorrow

★★★★ A GRE

50 CENTS

A WOND ARRIVES

By MICHAEL ESPOSITO

Boston residents were startled this morning by the sight of a woman in a patriotic red-and-blue outfit flying through the downtown business district. The Boston Police Department later reported that many of their precincts were flooded with phone calls reporting the strange occurrence. The woman was last seen flying south of Boston, over the Roxbury area.

This reporter had a personal sighting of the woman as she flew past a window on the eighteenth floor of the newspaper's offices on Haney Street at 9:24 this morning. She appeared to be approximately six feet tall with long, black hair. Her outfit consisted of a shiny, gold tiara on her head, a bright red tunic, star-spangled, blue shorts, and high, red boots. Above her tunic was an emblem that seemed to form the initials "W.W." This emblem prompted several people to dub her "Wonder Woman."

The origin of the flying woman remains a mystery. Some have speculated that she is advertising some patriotic product because of her flag-inspired outfit. Others are wondering if the woman is related to Superman, but the Man of Steel has so far not commented on the situation. In the past, Superman has explained that he is the only surviving member of his now-destroyed home planet of Krypton. The appearance of "Wonder Woman" though, has prompted many to wonder if superpowered visitors from other planets might visit Earth.

DIANA MADE HER PICTORIAL DEBUT IN THIS NEWSPAPER AND WAS ALSO NAMED "WONDER WOMAN" FOR THE FIRST TIME.

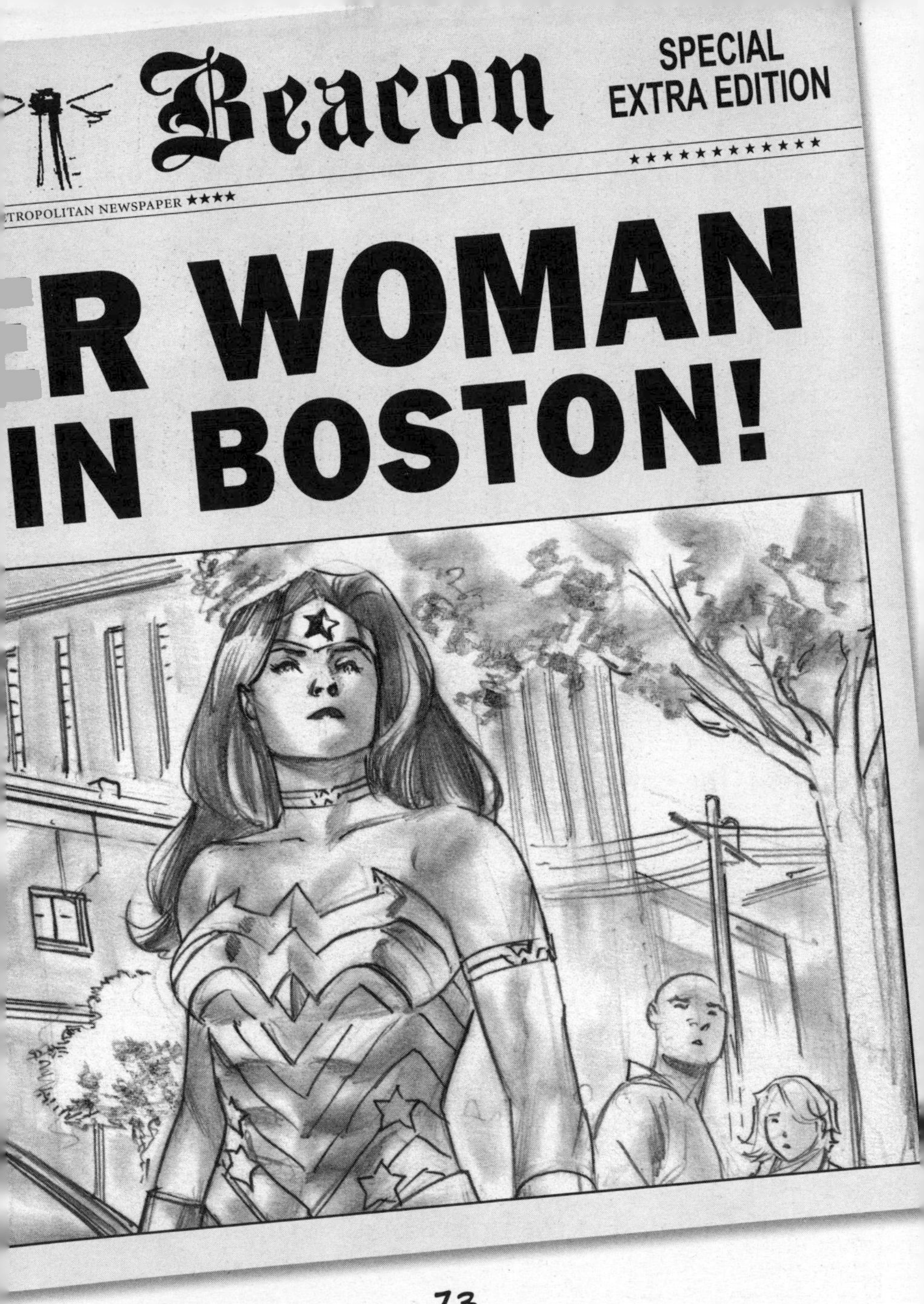
Beacon
SPECIAL
EXTRA EDITION
ETROPOLITAN NEWSPAPER ★★★★
R WOMAN
IN BOSTON!

"I have a lot to learn here in Man's World," Diana said to herself.

Diana planted her feet firmly on the ground and jumped in the air. The Greek god Hermes had given Diana the power of flight, and soon she was soaring high above the skyscrapers of Boston. As she flew past the offices of a Boston newspaper, one reporter happened to look out the window.

"What the—" the reporter sputtered. He quickly ran to his computer and started typing a story with this headline: A WONDER WOMAN ARRIVES IN BOSTON! Soon, the entire world would know Princess Diana of Themyscira as Wonder Woman!

Diana had returned Steve Trevor to his home. Now the most dangerous part of her mission would begin: to find Ares and prevent him from starting a nuclear war. On Themyscira, she had consulted with the wise Amazon Menalippe, who had told Diana where the largest collection of nuclear weapons could be found in the United States. Diana traveled to that military base and discovered that Ares was already there. The God of War had taken control of the mind of a soldier in the army. Ares had then locked that soldier behind the heavy steel door of the nuclear weapons control room. Ares was about to order the soldier to push the button that would launch a nuclear war and start World War III.

Diana flew as fast as she could and slammed into Ares, knocking over the enraged God of War.

"You are too late, Princess Diana!" he yelled. "I am about to give the command that will end mankind once and for all!"

As he stood up, Ares reached over and easily lifted Diana off the ground. He was about to throw her against the steel door.

Diana had to think quickly. She grabbed her Lasso of Truth and started swinging it high in the air. She then swiftly threw it around Ares so that he was caught within the lasso. The God of War cried out in pain and struggled against the golden ropes, but Diana held him tight.

Suddenly, Ares stopped moving. The Lasso of Truth caused him to realize what would happen if his evil plan succeeded. If all of Earth's humans were destroyed, there would be no one left for Ares to rule over or conquer. Without mankind's anger to help the God of War grow stronger, he would eventually disappear. Diana was astonished to see one tear falling from the God of War's eye!

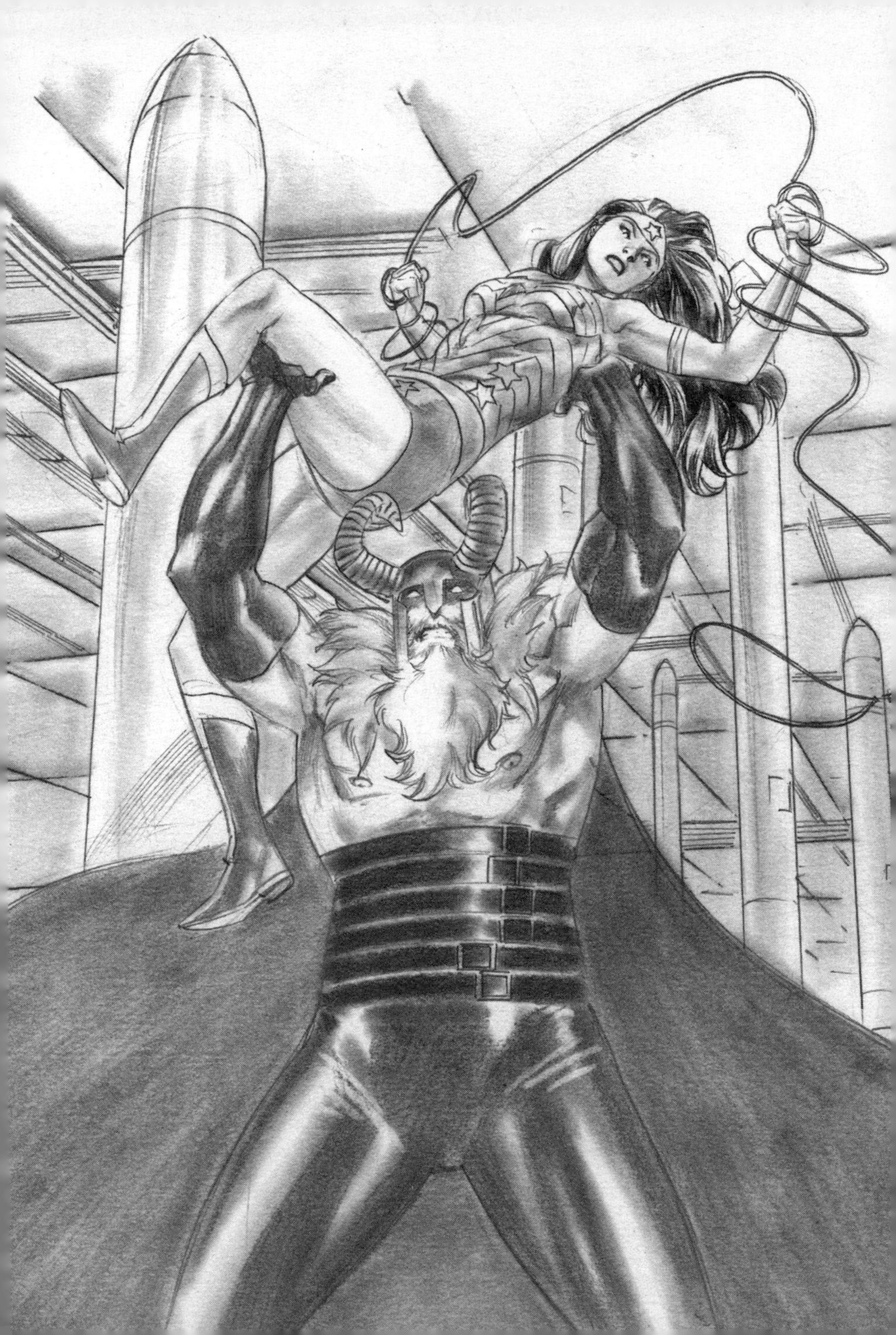

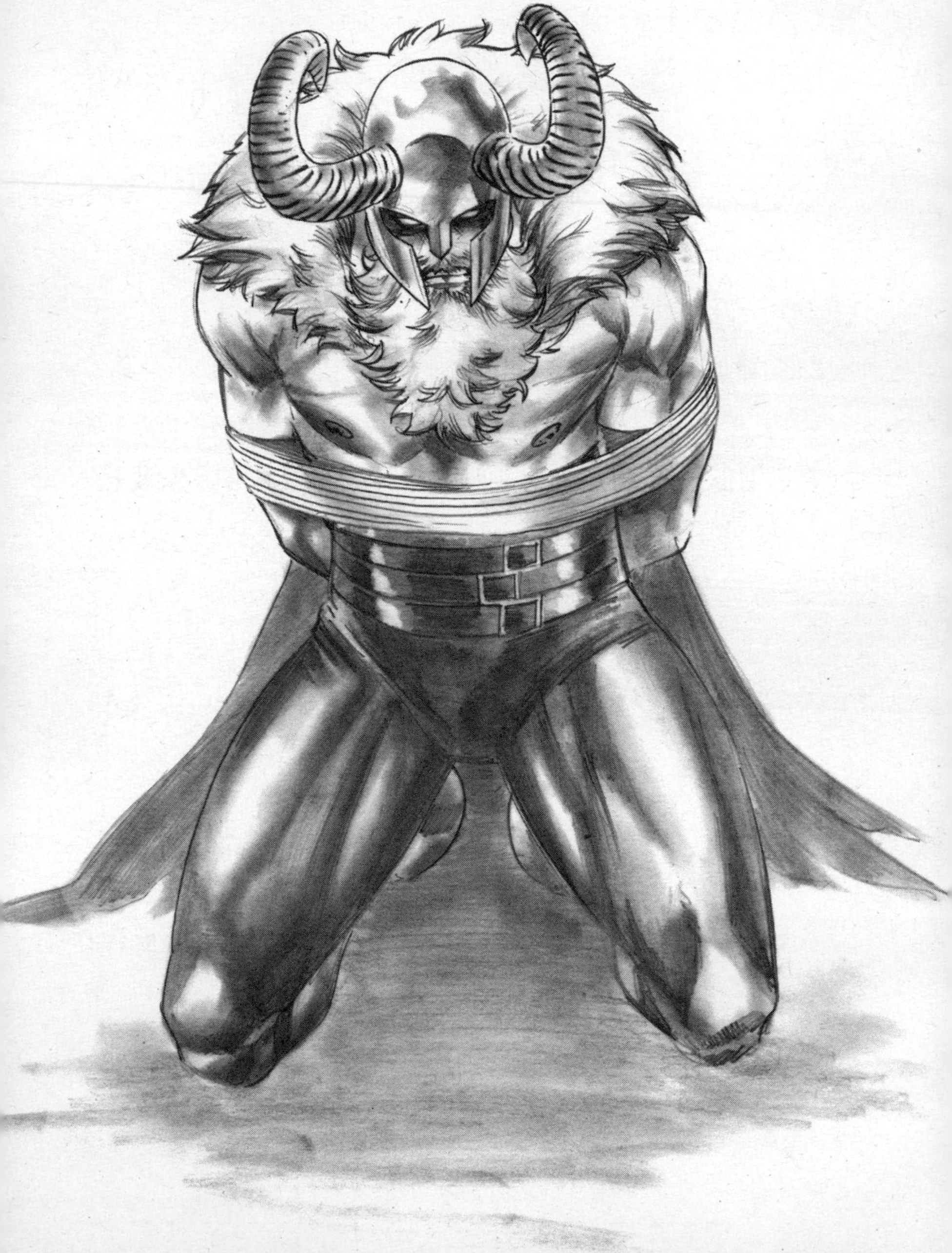

"I will not launch the nuclear missiles," Ares said. "But I am not finished. You can try to teach mankind the ways of peace. But I will continue to watch and grow stronger as the humans fight and go to war with one another. You and I will meet again, Princess!"

Diana removed the lasso from the God of War, and he vanished in a blast of smoke. Diana ripped open the steel door and freed the soldier. He had no memory of his actions while under Ares's control. Diana explained the situation, and the soldier thanked her for saving him. Without her help, he could have been responsible for the most terrible war the world had ever seen!

Diana had ended Ares's plot. Now she could begin her new mission as Wonder Woman: to fight for truth and justice in her new home and to inspire tolerance and compassion.

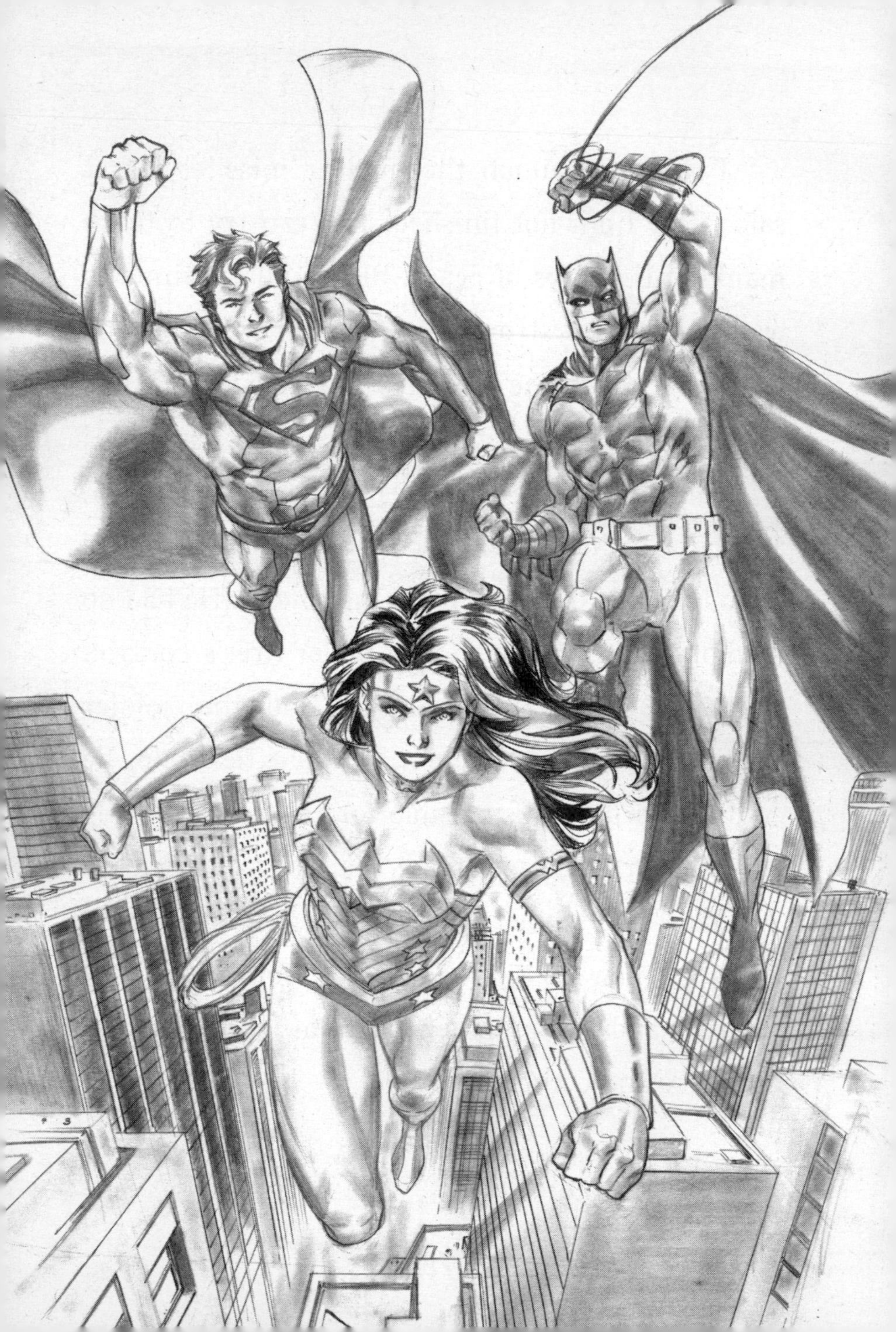

CHAPTER SEVEN

AWESOME ALLIES

Diana was chosen as the one Amazon to carry the messages of love and compassion from Paradise Island to the mortals of Earth. Although she often works alone, Diana has rarely been lonely. She has a long list of friends and allies who have helped her over the years.

At the top of that list is her mother, Queen Hippolyta, who guided the Amazons to their home on the island of Themyscira and has ruled wisely over them for 3,000 years. Hippolyta was a fierce warrior, but she chose to live a life devoted to peace and harmony instead of fighting. She loved her daughter and would do anything to protect her.

Princess Diana had a happy childhood on Paradise Island, surrounded by over a thousand Amazons who loved and guided her. Diana would be forever grateful to General Phillipus, who was Queen Hippolyta's closest advisor and the greatest Amazon warrior ever. General Phillipus trained the young princess in combat and also taught Diana how to control her amazing strength and powers. Once, during their training, Phillipus grew worried that Diana had become too confident in her abilities and was taking dangerous chances. Phillipus fired an arrow that wounded the princess, teaching Diana the valuable lesson that she was not invulnerable. It was thanks to General Phillipus that Diana became a skilled warrior who knew how to fight, and, perhaps more important, knew when *not* to fight!

HIPPOLYTA'S WISDOM AND STRENGTH ARE ALWAYS A SOURCE OF INSPIRATION FOR DIANA.

Mala

Mala was one of Princess Diana's closest friends among
the Amazons of Paradise Island. She was almost as skilled
as Diana in combat, and the two of them spent many
happy days in mock-battles. One time, Mala was attacked
by the flying Harpies, which were evil winged goddesses
with deadly claws. Diana bravely jumped on top of the
Harpy that was holding Mala and freed her friend from the
talons of the deadly beast.

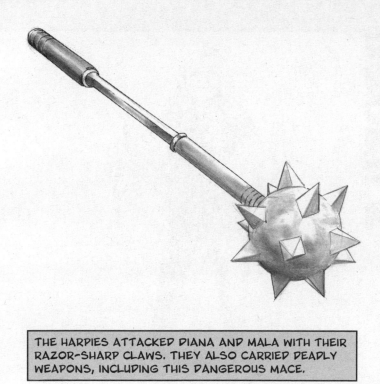

THE HARPIES ATTACKED DIANA AND MALA WITH THEIR RAZOR-SHARP CLAWS. THEY ALSO CARRIED DEADLY WEAPONS, INCLUDING THIS DANGEROUS MACE.

Diana was the first and only child born on Themyscira, and sometimes she wished that she could play with someone her own age. To give the princess a childhood friend, the Amazon sorceress Magala magically brought Diana's own reflection in a mirror to life. Magala created a duplicate of Diana and named her Donna. Diana now had a twin sister! Together, the two young princesses wrestled, swam,

Wonder Girl

She is not an Amazon, but she is a hero and a member of the crime-fighting team known as the Teen Titans. Cassandra "Cassie" Sandsmark was the daughter of an archaeologist, and it was during an expedition in Cambodia that Cassie discovered two ancient bracelets that transformed her clothes into protective armor and created a silver lasso. The press named her "Wonder Girl," a name she dislikes.

and played together from dawn until dusk. All too soon, though, Diana lost her playmate when the villainous Dark Angel kidnapped Donna, mistakenly

DIANA WEARS THIS TIARA TO SHOW THAT SHE IS THE PRINCESS OF THEMYSCIRA. WITH ITS RAZOR-SHARP EDGES, THE TIARA IS ALSO AN EFFECTIVE WEAPON THAT DIANA CAN THROW AT HER ENEMIES.

thinking that she had taken Diana. Years later, Diana and Donna were reunited, and Donna joined Wonder Woman in her fight against evildoers.

Another famous Amazon was briefly known as Wonder Woman. Her name was Artemis, and she would become one of Diana's closest allies. Centuries ago, the Amazons had two queens: Hippolyta and Antiope. Hippolyta and her fellow Amazons chose to make their home on Themyscira, where they would live forever. Antiope and her followers took the name Bana-Mighdall and became the "Lost Tribe of Amazons," moving to a hidden city in Egypt. When they did this, they were not blessed with immortality like the Amazons.

AFTER ANTIOPE DIED, THE LOST TRIBE WAS LED BY MANY FIERCE WARRIORS, INCLUDING ARTEMIS THE HUNTER.

Years after Diana had traveled to Man's World, she journeyed to the secret home of the Bana-Mighdall and discovered that a fierce redheaded warrior named Artemis was leading them. Although the Amazons and Bana-Mighdall had many differences, they fought together in battles and afterward decided to join forces on Themyscira.

Many years later, Hippolyta was told that Diana's life was in danger. The queen called for a new contest to determine who was best qualified to serve as Wonder Woman. Although Artemis did not possess super-strength, she defeated Diana in the contest and briefly served as Wonder Woman. Sadly, Artemis lacked Diana's talents for compassion or diplomacy, and her violent temper led to her downfall in a battle with the White Magician. Diana regained the title of Wonder Woman and helped Artemis to escape from her imprisonment.

On Themyscira, Diana learned the value of teamwork from her fellow Amazons. When she

ARTEMIS DEFEATED DIANA TO WIN THE TITLE OF WONDER WOMAN FOR A TIME.

WONDER WOMAN SAVED SUPERMAN'S LIFE BY DEFEATING MAXWELL LORD.

arrived in the world of mortals, it was no surprise that she was invited to become a member of the world's greatest team of Super Heroes, the Justice League. Her powerful teammates included Superman, Batman, Green Lantern, Martian Manhunter, Aquaman, and The Flash. The Justice League has journeyed to distant galaxies and even traveled through time to fight some of the most dangerous villains in the universe. Diana is always ready to help her teammates. One time, she saved Superman when the villainous Maxwell Lord was controlling the Man of Steel's mind. Diana threw her Lasso of Truth around Lord and forced him to reveal how to save Superman.

Batman has great admiration for Wonder Woman's skills as a warrior and frequently trains with her in the Justice League's headquarters. Batman's dark and gloomy personality, though, could not be more different from Diana's optimism and love of life. One of her most unusual partnerships occurred when

BATMAN LOVES SPARRING WITH A PARTNER WHO CAN MATCH HIS MARTIAL ARTS SKILLS BLOW FOR BLOW.

she teamed up with the Dark Knight. It happened when the three children of Ares arrived in Gotham City and took control of Poison Ivy, the Scarecrow, and the Joker. Even worse, Batman's mind was taken over by Phobos, the God of Fear. Wonder Woman helped Batman to drive out the evil spirit of Phobos, and together they defeated Ares's children.

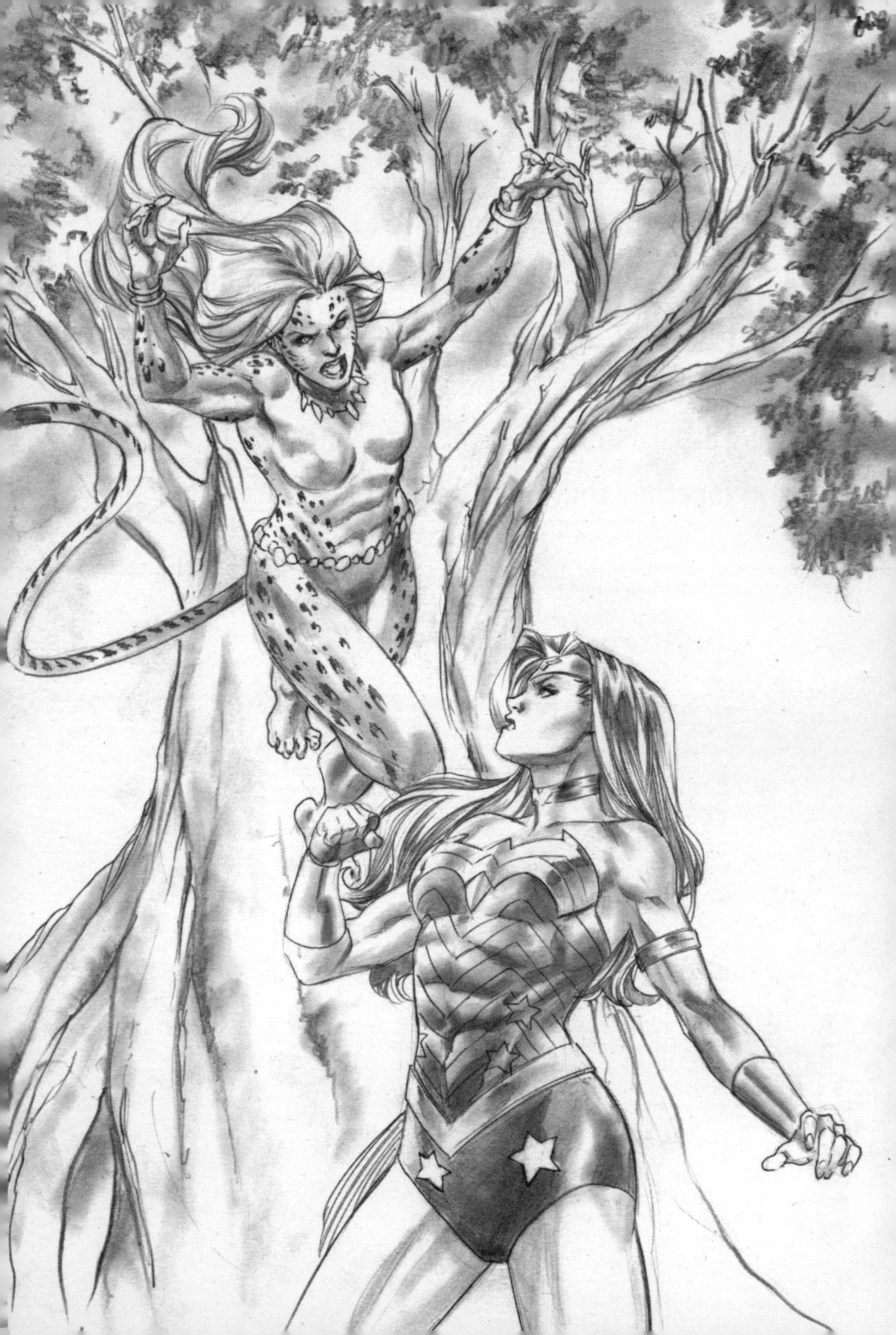

CHAPTER EIGHT

FEARSOME FOES

When Diana traveled from Themyscira to Man's World, her first goal was to defeat Ares. After she stopped the God of War from starting a nuclear war, Diana hoped to spend most of her time working as an ambassador from Paradise Island, helping the rest of the world to adopt the Amazons' message of peace. Unfortunately, a deadly collection of villains, demons, and monsters had other plans.

Even Ares was not quiet for long. This brutal

villain is the son of the Greek god Zeus, and over the centuries he has also been known as Mars and the God of War. Ares was bitterly opposed to the creation of the peace-loving Amazons, and he has fought them throughout their entire history. He is a master of weaponry, and he never hesitates to use violence to achieve his goals. Nothing would make Ares happier than to see all the humans of Earth plunged into warfare. He was furious to be defeated by Wonder Woman and has vowed to destroy her and all the Amazons. Ares is one of the most powerful villains that Wonder Woman has ever faced.

Circe is an ancient and powerful magician who uses her spells for evil purposes. She can live forever and has caused problems for the Amazons for centuries. Circe was responsible for the death of Queen Antiope, who was Hippolyta's sister and the leader of the Bana-Mighdall tribe of Amazons. Circe has the ability to transform men into dangerous animals known as Bestiamorphs, and she can then

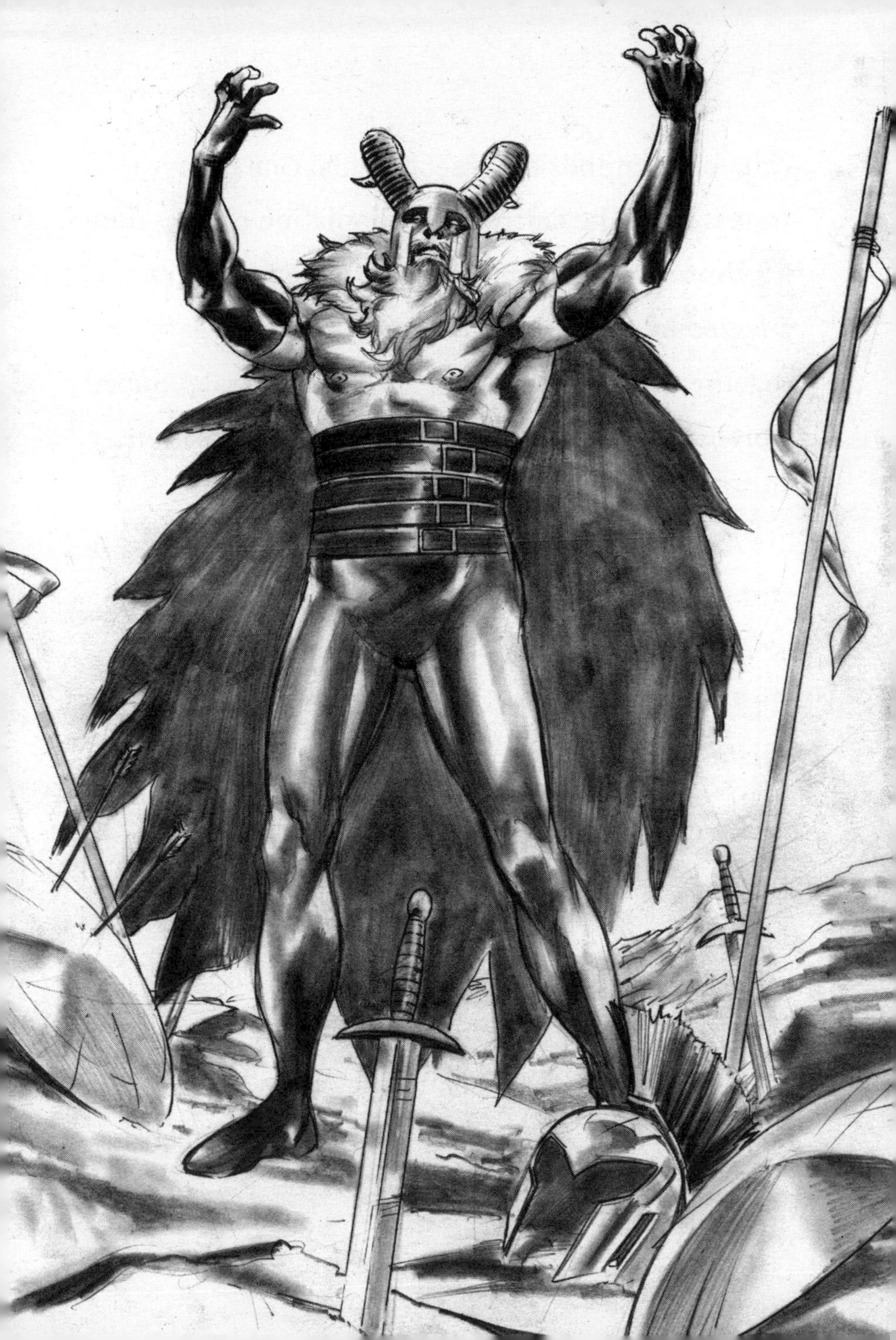

control the minds of these animals. One time, Circe transformed the entire male population of New York City into Bestiamorphs. Because women were not affected by Circe's magic, Wonder Woman gathered together many of Earth's greatest female Super Heroes to fight the villain and break Circe's spell.

CIRCE'S POWERFUL MAGIC MAKES HER A TERRIFYING FOE!

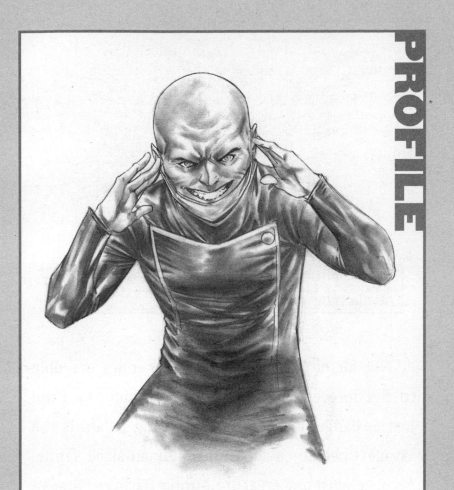

Doctor Psycho

Doctor Psycho is one of Wonder Woman's smallest opponents, but that doesn't make him any less dangerous. This medical madman is able to control the minds of others, and he often attacks his victims while they are dreaming. He dislikes all women and especially hates Wonder Woman.

URZKARTAGA IS THE NAME OF THE DEADLY AFRICAN PLANT THAT TRANSFORMED BARBARA MINERVA INTO THE CHEETAH.

Not all of Wonder Woman's enemies are able to live forever, but many of her human foes are just as dangerous. Another terrifying villain is the savage Cheetah, a ferocious, human-sized feline. Archaeologist and treasure hunter Barbara Minerva was traveling through Africa on a safari when she discovered a dangerous, blood-drinking plant. When Minerva swallowed some of the plant, she was transformed into the bloodthirsty Cheetah. While under the plant's influence, Minerva grows razor-sharp claws and acquires cat-like reflexes and the strength of a giant feline. She can even use her long cat-like tail to strangle her opponents!

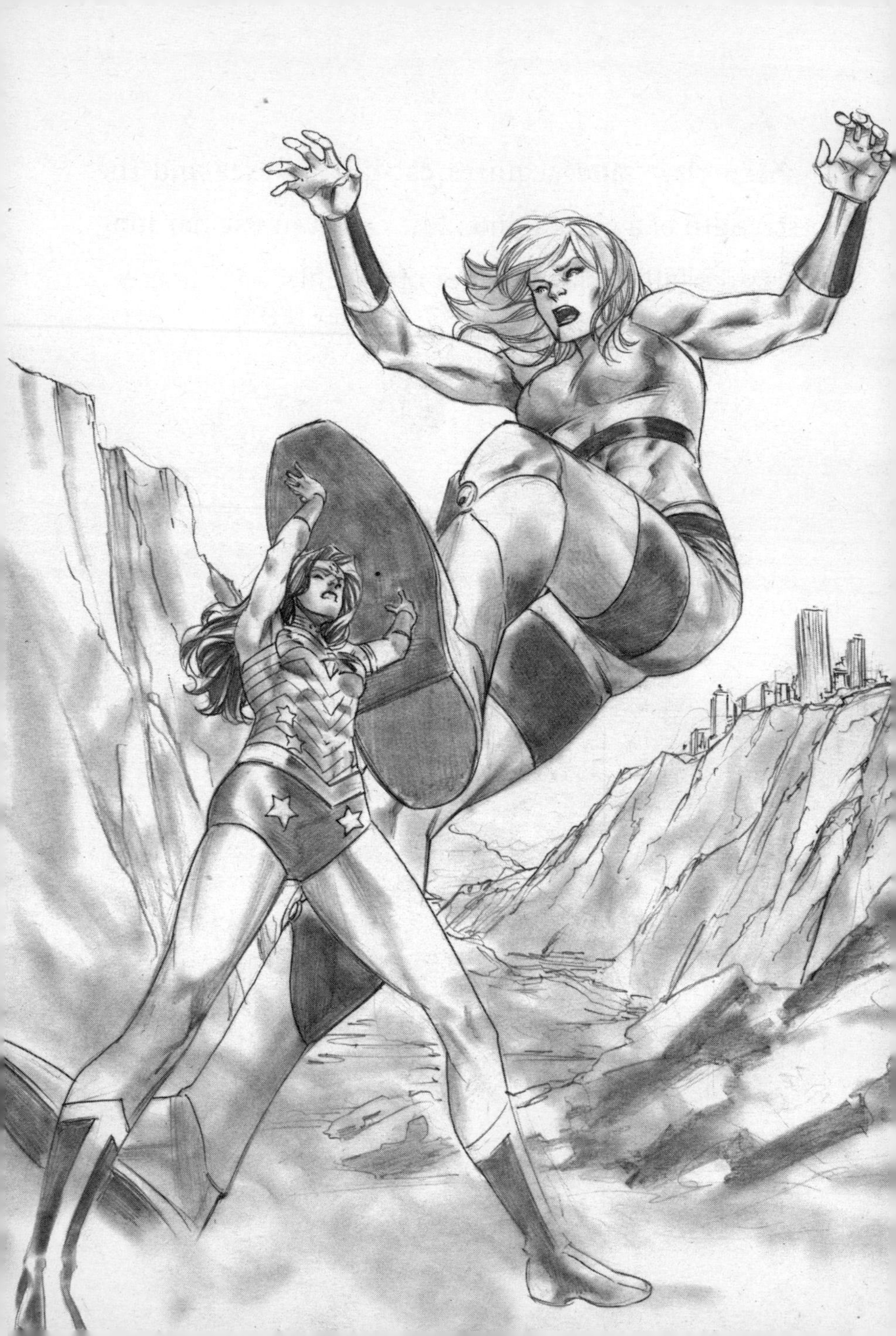

In size alone, the hundred-foot-tall villain Giganta is one of Wonder Woman's largest opponents. Giganta was originally a brilliant doctor named Doris Zeul, who was dying from a rare blood disease. Dr. Zeul came up with a crazy plan to transfer her mind into Wonder Woman's body, but a lab assistant instead placed her mind into the body of a giant gorilla known as Giganta. In her new gorilla body, Zeul kidnapped a circus strongwoman named Olga, and she then managed to transfer her mind into Olga's body. Zeul was now able to grow to a towering height. She has the body of a giant human, the mind of a brilliant villain, and the power of a super-sized gorilla. Diana needs all her strength when she confronts this towering foe.

There is another dangerous doctor on the list of Wonder Woman's enemies. She is Doctor Poison, who is an expert on poisons, viruses, and dangerous chemicals. Deadly poisons have no effect on this villain, and sometimes she can spread a virus just

Devastation

Although Devastation is only twelve years old, she is a deadly enemy who shares many of Wonder Woman's powers. The Greek god Cronus hated Wonder Woman so much that he created his daughter Devastation out of the same clay that formed Princess Diana. Unlike Diana's mission to bring peace and love to the world, Devastation's goal is to bring unhappiness and violence. There was one small drop of goodness in the clay that formed Devastation, and Diana's only hope is to appeal to the tiny bit of kindness in Devastation.

by opening her mouth. Doctor Poison created the deadly Pandora Virus by using some blood from Wonder Woman's foe Devastation. Victims that were exposed to this virus were transformed into horrible monsters. Fortunately, Wonder Woman was able to reverse the effects of the plague and bring Doctor Poison to justice.

DOCTOR POISON ISN'T A STRONG FIGHTER. SHE PREFERS TO LET HER TOXINS DO HER DIRTY WORK.

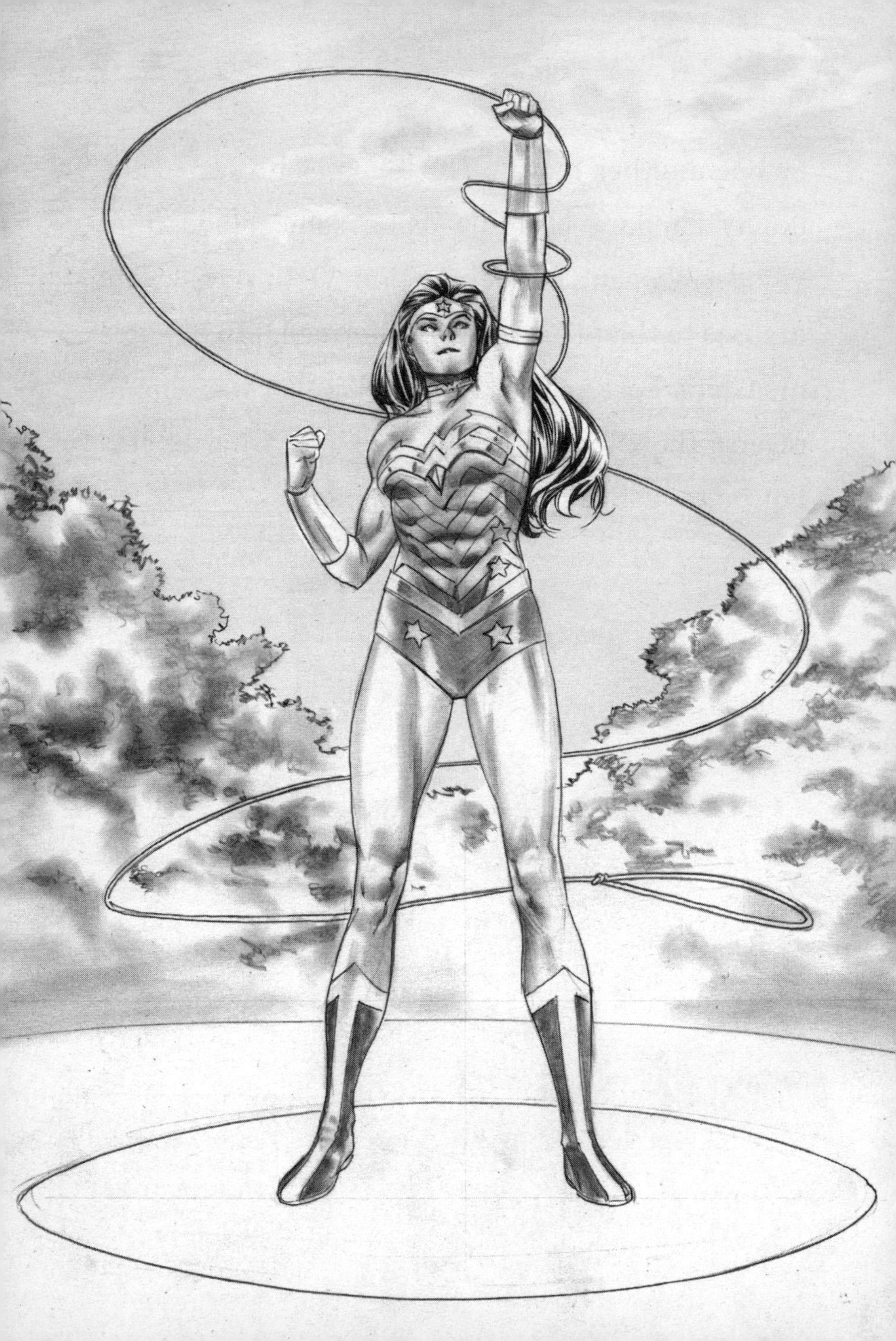

THE AMAZING
AMAZON

Diana was born a princess in a society of peaceful women. She came to our world on a mission to protect mankind and promote harmony. As Wonder Woman, she is one of the most powerful heroes on earth.

Diana departed from Themyscira with an amazing array of powers, including the ability to fly. Sometimes, though, she needs a vehicle to travel into outer space or to transport others. Soon after she became Wonder Woman, she acquired one of

WONDER WOMAN IS A POWERFUL SPEAKER. SHE KNOWS THAT A
CALL TO ACTION CAN CHANGE THE WORLD AS MUCH AS ANY FIGHT.

her most wonderful powers: the ability to create an Invisible Jet. An alien race called the Lansanarians gave Diana a special crystal that could morph into any shape. Using just her mind, Diana could use the crystal to create amazing transparent vehicles, including a giant Invisible Jet.

The Invisible Jet is based on the designs of Amazon engineers, and it can travel at twenty times the speed of sound. With a single thought, Diana has the power to morph the jet into a transparent motorcycle, submarine, or even a horse-drawn chariot.

Every day brings a new adventure to Diana. One day, you will find her in her Amazonian robes addressing the United Nations in her role as an ambassador from Themyscira. On the next day, you will find her meeting her fellow Justice League members in the team's floating headquarters known as the Watchtower. On another day, she will be battling the giant villain Giganta, trying to knock

DIANA HAS THE POWER TO FLY, BUT SOMETIMES SHE NEEDS A VEHICLE TO TRAVEL INTO OUTER SPACE OR TO TRANSPORT OTHERS.

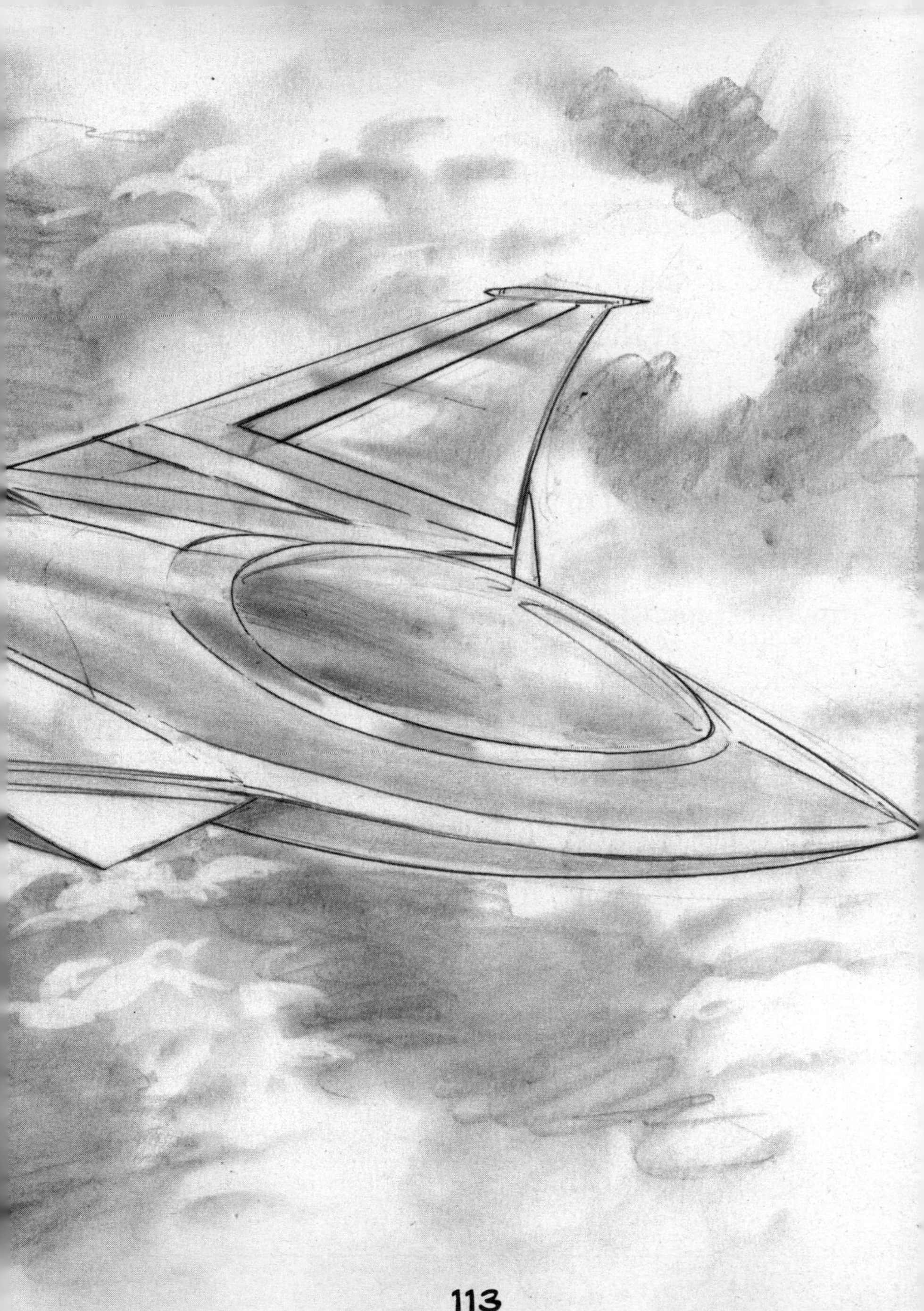

her down to the ground. It's just a normal week for the Amazing Amazon.

Ares is one of Wonder Woman's most dangerous enemies, and she has battled the God of War many times. But Ares is not the only one of Wonder Woman's famous foes who has returned over and over, determined to cause trouble for Diana.

The magician Circe brought back to life the mythical monster known as the Medusa, a horrible

WHENEVER THE WORLD IS IN DANGER, DIANA CAN COUNT ON HER FRIENDS IN THE JUSTICE LEAGUE TO BACK HER UP.

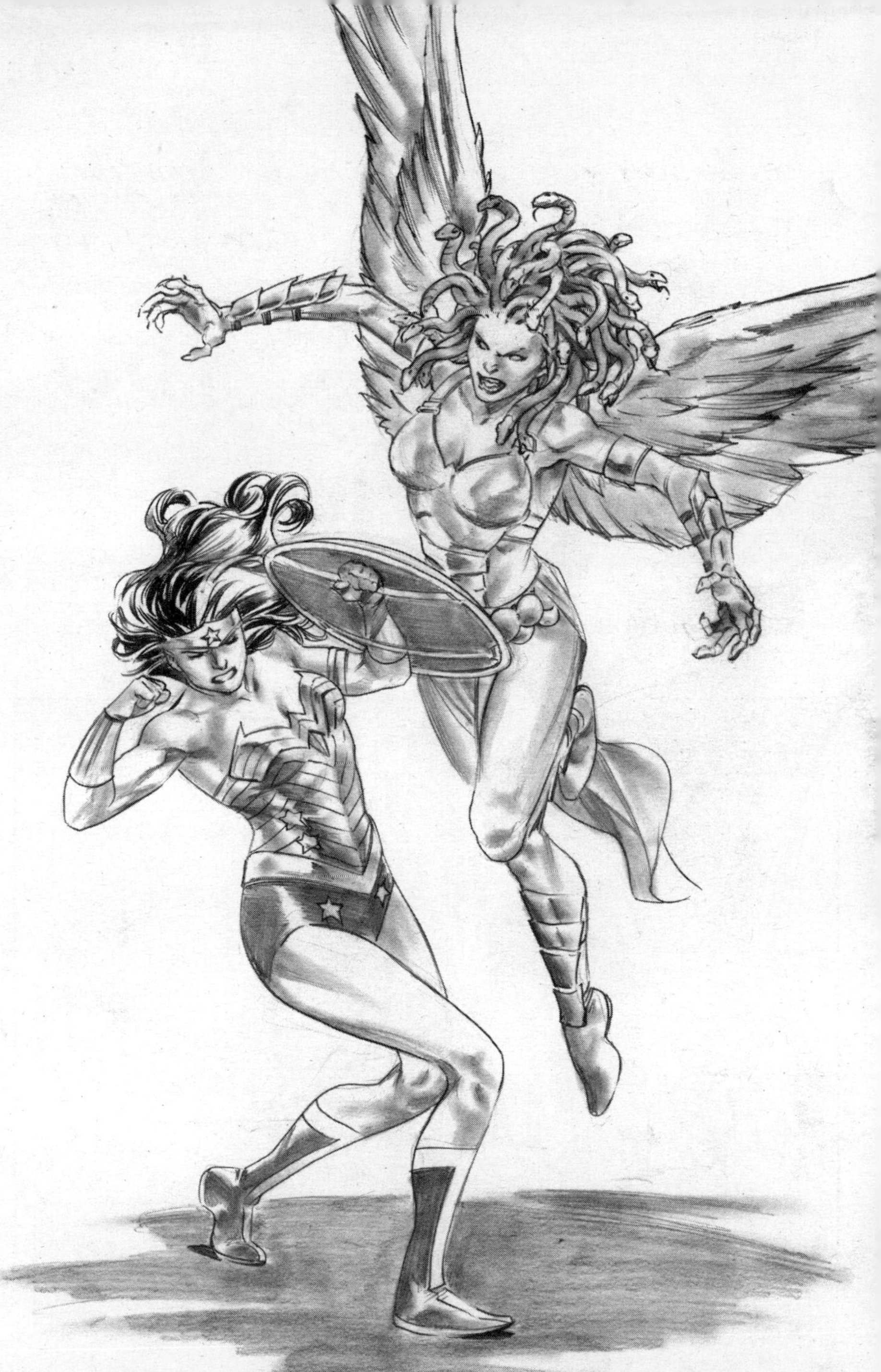

IMPERIEX HAS EXISTED SINCE THE BEGINNING OF THE UNIVERSE. HE IS OBSESSED WITH BRINGING ORDER TO "CHAOTIC" WORLDS LIKE EARTH.

creature with snakes for hair. Just one look into Medusa's eyes could have turned Diana to stone, but the Amazon princess covered her eyes and jumped over a cliff to stop the monster from hurting others. Years later, Circe put a magical spell on Diana that temporarily turned her into a mortal. Diana continued to fight criminals, proving that she was still a hero even without her powers.

Diana has fought at the side of some of the most powerful heroes in the galaxy. When an alien known as Imperiex and the computerized monster Brainiac 13 threatened the entire universe, she joined forces with Superman and other heroes to battle the foes. During that fight, the Amazon's island home of Themyscira was destroyed, but the Amazons rebuilt it.

Wonder Woman is a hero who can conquer with force, but her first instinct is always to seek justice through peaceful means.

She learned the values of wisdom, strength,

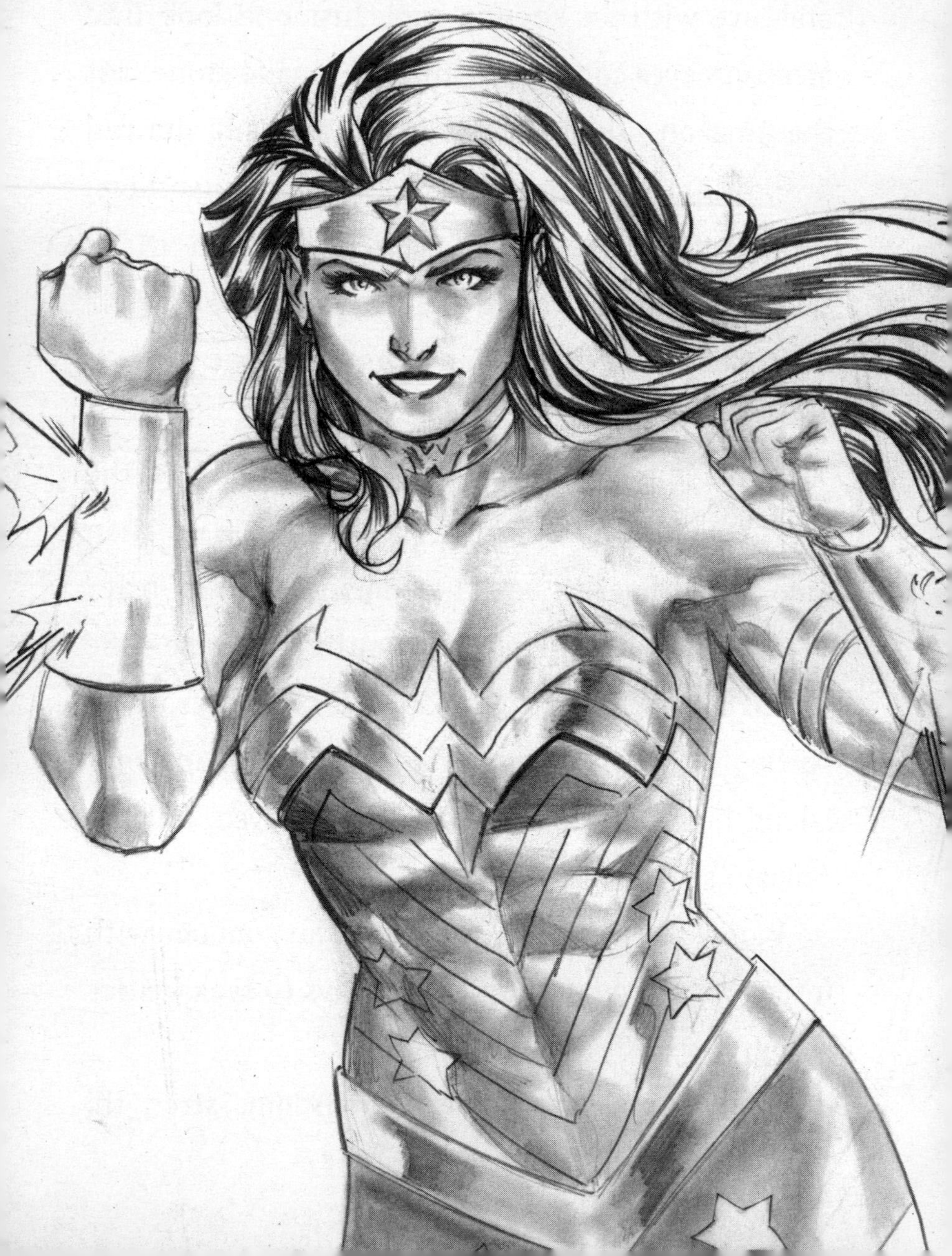

and love from the Amazons on Paradise Island. The Amazons sent Diana on a mission to change a world that was filled with hatred and wars. She did not hesitate to accept that challenge, and she has never stopped protecting the innocent or fighting evil.

She is strong, fearless, and compassionate.

She is Wonder Woman!

Fast Facts

W Wonder Woman is as strong as Superman.

W Diana was trained by the Amazons to become an expert in martial arts, and she is easily as skilled as Batman.

W She used the secret identity of "Diana Prince" when she worked for the Department of Metahuman Affairs.

W She can fly faster than the speed of sound.

W Diana can use her silver bracelets to deflect bullets.

W Wonder Woman's golden Lasso of Truth is practically indestructible.

W Her tiara can be thrown like a boomerang. It is so sharp that it can also be used as a cutting instrument.

Diana can communicate with animals, and she is able to calm the most ferocious beasts.

 Diana is able to use her mind to create countless invisible vehicles, including a jet, a motorcycle, and even a horse-drawn chariot.

 Wonder Woman and Superman were photographed kissing, which quickly led to rumors of a romantic relationship.

 Centuries before Diana was born, the Amazons on Paradise Island rode giant kangaroo-like creatures called Sky Kangas. The animals are now extinct.

 No mortal or god can escape from Wonder Woman's golden Lasso of Truth.

☰ Diana is able to spin in place so quickly that no one can see her change from her civilian clothing into her Wonder Woman uniform.

☰ The shape-shifting criminal Clayface usually battles Batman, but when the gooey villain touched Wonder Woman he absorbed some of her godlike powers.

☰ Donna Troy fought crime as the hero Troia, and her amazing costume was filled with actual shining stars.

☰ Once, when Diana was running low on money, she took a job as a waitress at Taco Whiz.

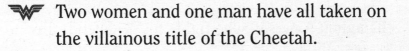 When Artemis briefly replaced Diana as Wonder Woman, Diana switched to a black costume. It had stars on it so that Diana could continue to honor the memory of Diana Trevor.

One time, all of the gods of Olympus were turned to stone. Wonder Woman brought all the gods back to life, even her enemy Ares.

Two women and one man have all taken on the villainous title of the Cheetah.

Themyscira is hidden in the center of the Bermuda Triangle.

Glossary

advisor: Someone who helps important people make decisions.

ambassador: A messenger sent to a different country or place to represent his or her homeland.

ancient: Someone or something that is very old.

archaeologist: Someone who studies the ancient past.

champion: A person who fights for or defends any person or cause.

chronology: A list of events in order of when they happened.

debut: The first public appearance of someone or something.

immortality: The state of living forever.

imprisonment: The state of being trapped in a single location.

indestructible: Something that cannot be hurt or taken apart.

predict: To see or guess the future before it happens.

philosophy: The system of principles that guides someone in all their choices.

rival: Someone who is competing for the same goal or object as someone else.

secluded: To be far away from most people.

test pilot: Someone who flies planes to check them for speed and safety.